Prais

A LIFE
OF WORSHIP

Rich deposits of talent, training and anointing have created a worship leader of extraordinary measure in David Morris. Now, he has penned for the Body of Christ to read and comprehend that which he lives to demonstrate—worship of the Almighty.

Dennis and Patti Amsden
FOUNDERS AND PASTORS, SON LIFE CHURCH
COLLINSVILLE, ILLINOIS

A Lifestyle of Worship is a must read for all God seekers. In this excellent book, David Morris focuses on the principles of worship essential to connecting with God on a meaningful, personal level each day.

LaMar Boschman
DEAN, THE WORSHIP INSTITUTE
BEDFORD, TEXAS

With great delight I recommend to you *A Lifestyle of Worship.* David Morris is not only a gifted musician, but he also lives out the message he so eloquently conveys in this book. In it, David captures God's passionate and loving heart for His people. As a worship leader, I plan to keep this book close by for the growth of my ministry—and my heart.

Chris DuPré
SENIOR WORSHIP LEADER, METRO CHRISTIAN FELLOWSHIP
KANSAS CITY, MISSOURI

David Morris speaks out of experience and from his heart, with transparency and pure simplicity. Worship is a lifestyle, not just an emotion; it is a conviction, an act of the will. *A Lifestyle of Worship* is a good practical tool for all worshipers.

Frank Damazio
PASTOR, CITY BIBLE CHURCH, FORMERLY BIBLE TEMPLE
PORTLAND, OREGON

With a keen sense of history and a broad theological perspective, David Morris summons us to walk the most exciting "highway" mankind can know: the journey of encountering God. The throb of personal devotion, the practice of corporate worship and the relevance of current prophetic revelation are masterfully interwoven in this work. *A Lifestyle of Worship* is sure to become a standard in contemporary worship literature.

Steven Fry
PRESIDENT, MESSENGER FELLOWSHIP
AUTHOR OF *A GOD WHO HEALS THE HEART*
BRENTWOOD, TENNESSEE

An excellent book! David Morris skillfully weaves together autobiographical, theological and historical threads into a beautiful garment of praise for the believer and the Body of Christ! David's heart for God and for His church is powerfully revealed in these pages.

Jim Hodges
APOSTOLIC TEAM LEADER
FEDERATION OF MINISTERS AND CHURCHES, INC.
DUNCANVILLE, TEXAS

Praise for

A LIFESTYLE
OF WORSHIP

This is a must-read book. We need more teaching on worship, both in the prayer movement and the Church, and David Morris is a pioneer in the area of prophetic worship. His book will lead us to more intimate relationship with the Father, both personally and corporately.

Cindy Jacobs
AUTHOR, *WOMEN OF DESTINY*
COLORADO SPRINGS, COLORADO

David Morris has done his homework in heaven and on earth. You will find life-transforming insights throughout *A Lifestyle of Worship*. Don't read it too quickly.

Michael Mass
PASTOR, CHURCH OF THE KING
DALLAS, TEXAS

A Lifestyle of Worship is a work of intimacy. David Morris opens his life to us and invites us to let his spiritual journey become our own. He takes us into his sanctuary and teaches us how to enter into the full expression of personal and congregational worship. Every believer needs an understanding of the truths in this book.

Ross Parsley
WORSHIP PASTOR, NEW LIFE CHURCH
COLORADO SPRINGS, COLORADO

Praise for

A LIFESTYLE
of WORSHIP

Through Adam and Eve, the Lord revealed his restorative plan by a
sacrificial lifestyle of worship. This plan has been passed from
generation to generation. *A Lifestyle of Worship* captures that
heritage of worship for this generation. David Morris reveals God's
heart and nature to draw us near to Himself. Enter into a new
dimension of expression and understanding of Psalms 149 and 150.
Let the Lord use this book to help you become a true worshiper!

Chuck Pierce
DIRECTOR, WORLD PRAYER CENTER
COLORADO SPRINGS, COLORADO

In his own living-room conversational style, David Morris
thoughtfully guides us from the personal passions of worship to
the corporate expressions of congregational praise. With gripping
transparency he traces the landmarks of his personal pilgrimage
toward authentic, grace-empowered intimacy with God.
A Lifestyle of Worship will gently remind you of the Father's
search for relationship, and will renew your pursuit of the highest
calling—ministering unto the Lord.

Bob Sorge
PASTOR, ZION FELLOWSHIP
AUTHOR OF *EXPLORING WORSHIP* AND *IN HIS FACE*
CANANDAIGUA, NEW YORK

In the circle of Christian leaders I am closest to, the name at the top of the list of those who understand "prophetic worship" is David Morris. With clarity and passion, David will help you to understand worship and experience true intimacy with God. I am thrilled with *A Lifestyle of Worship*.

C. Peter Wagner
PROFESSOR, FULLER THEOLOGICAL SEMINARY
COLORADO SPRINGS, COLORADO

We know that today's postmodern persons are longing for a deeper spiritual experience. David Morris bypasses the superficialities of warm, fuzzy feelings and gives concrete meaning to what the truly spiritual experience of worship looks like. *A Lifestyle of Worship* is an important book for your own spiritual journey.

Robert Webber
DIRECTOR, INSTITUTE FOR WORSHIP STUDIES
WHEATON, ILLINOIS

A LIFESTYLE of WORSHIP

Making Your Life a Daily Offering

DAVID MORRIS

Renew

A Division of Gospel Light
Ventura, California, U.S.A.

Published by Renew Books
A Division of Gospel Light
Ventura, California, U.S.A.
Printed in U.S.A.

Renew Books is a ministry of Gospel Light, an evangelical Christian publisher dedicated
to serving the local church. We believe God's vision for Gospel Light is to provide
church leaders with biblical, user-friendly materials that will help them evangelize,
disciple and minister to children, youth and families.

It is our prayer that this Renew book will help you discover biblical truth for your
own life and help you meet the needs of others. May God richly bless you.

*For a free catalog of resources from Renew Books and Gospel Light please call your
Christian supplier, or contact us at* 1-800-4-GOSPEL *or at* www.gospellight.com.

All Scripture quotations, unless otherwise indicated, are taken from the the the *New American
Standard Bible,* © 1960, 1962, 1963, 1968, 1971, 1972, 1973, 1975, 1977 by The Lockman Foundation.
Used by permission.

Other versions used are:
AMP. N.T.—Scripture quotations are taken from the *Amplified New Testament,* copyright ©
1954, 1958, 1987 by The Lockman Foundation. Used by permission.
AMP. O.T.—From *The Amplified Bible, Old Testament.* Copyright © 1965, 1987 by The
Zondervan Corporation. Used by permission.
NIV—From the *Holy Bible, New International Version* ®. *NIV* ®. Copyright © 1973, 1978, 1984
by International Bible Society. Used by permission of Zondervan Publishing House. All rights
reserved.
The Message—© 1994 by Eugene Peterson. Published by NavPress.

Lyrics from contemporary songs used by permission.

Cover Design by Kevin Keller
Interior Design by Robert Williams
Edited by Karen Kaufman

LIBRARY OF CONGRESS CATALOGING-IN-PUBLICATION DATA
Morris, David, 1959—
A lifestyle of worship / David Morris.
    p. cm.
Includes bibliographical references.
ISBN 0-8307-2199-1 (pbk.)
1. God—Worship and love. I. Title.
BV4817.M67 1998   98-40567
248.3—dc21   CIP

1 2 3 4 5 6 7 8 9 10 11 12 13 14 15 / 04 03 02 01 00 99 98

Rights for publishing this book in other languages are contracted by Gospel Literature
International (GLINT). GLINT also provides technical help for the adaptation, translation and
publishing of Bible study resources and books in scores of languages worldwide. For further
information, write to GLINT at P.O. Box 4060, Ontario, CA 91761-1003, U.S.A. You may also
send e-mail to Glintint@aol.com, or visit their web site at www.glint.org.

I dedicate this book...

To my partner in life and cherished treasure, Laurie. You've not just stood by me, but with me in the heights and depths of life's many seasons. I will always be intrigued by your grace and forever grateful for your selfless love and support! You've contributed a great deal to this book through your prayers and the family stability you maintained through it all. I owe you the world,...and a vacation!

To my parents, Milton and Phyllis Morris. Thank you for creating and nurturing in me a "God consciousness." I will always remember the sacrifices you made to keep our family focused on the eternal realm during an era filled with the mockery of God. May the product of my life's story in this book bless and honor you as vessels of God's grace to me.

To "the Father of mercies and God of all comfort; who comforts us in all our affliction so that we may be able to comfort those who are in any affliction" (2 Cor. 1:3). May Your healing balm saturate all who partake of Your divine nature through true worship!

CONTENTS

FOREWORD

I have had the pleasure of calling David Morris my friend for 17 years. We have watched each other establish homes, raise kids, play games, laugh, cry, pray, worship, grow from "boys of God" to "men of God" and struggle our way into fairly successful national and international ministries. Our journeys, like most, have known the paradoxes of pain and pleasure, brokenness and blessing. David and I are much more than acquaintances. We have shared a lot of living.

I owe much to this God-given relationship. David has modeled for me honesty, integrity, perseverance, worship, family values, transparency, humility, repentance, a willingness to change and many other noble and godly character traits. Having served in a local church context with him for the past 12 years, David holds a very special distinction in my life. More times than any other human being, he has ushered me into the place I cherish most—the presence of God.

I have watched David lead worship in small prayer meetings, retreats, local church settings and international conferences. The skill with which he weaves a theme into the worship experience, his sensitivity at discerning and flowing with the moods of the Spirit and his remarkable ability to move a group of people as one into the presence of God all lend themselves to the same conclusion: David Morris is an amazing gift to the Body of Christ.

It is right, and I'm sure the wisdom of God, that a much broader portion of the Church now has the benefit of feeding on his rich insights through his book. With any new move of the Holy Spirit certain voices that God has held back in His school of preparation come to the forefront and become instructors and pacesetters for the new and fresh. David Morris is one of those voices.

Through this book you're about to move into more than a teaching. You're being afforded the privilege of stepping into the fruit of another person's journey. The difference is profound. Some practice what they preach, others preach what they practice. David is the latter. Lessons born of study can be enlightening. Lessons born of life can be life changing. Get ready to be changed! As you move with David through his personal struggles toward intimacy with God, I can assure you that you'll find yourself mirrored in the pages. You'll identify with the frustration of his daily devotions, and find great hope in his discovery of a God who asks not for our performance, but the pleasure of our daily walk with Him.

New and powerful vitality will fill the corporate worship experience as the rich insights God has given David come to life in these pages. For this reason alone, every believer in Christ should read this book. We live in a day of unprecedented amounts of information and revelation. With so much available teaching, so many "how to" conferences and seminars, we run the risk of thinking we can methodize everything, including our relationship with God. We are extremely gifted at complicating the simple. Knowing this, the Lord instructed in 2 Corinthians 11:3 not to be "led astray from the simplicity and purity of devotion to Christ." Indeed our depth of revelation in other areas of truth does not diminish the need for simple, pure devotion to Christ. In fact it increases it. The larger the tree, the deeper must go the roots. Likewise, the more we spread ourselves upward and outward into the multidimensional aspects of the Kingdom, the more we must allow the decomplicating effects of our relationship with Christ to go downward.

Perhaps the highest compliment I can pay *A Lifestyle of Worship* is that it will help you do this. With great eloquence and remarkable clarity, David Morris has demonstrated that profoundness need not be confusing, and relationship with Jesus can be fun, easy and daily. Thank you, David, for this labor of love!

Dutch Sheets
Colorado Springs, Colorado

ACKNOWLEDGMENTS

With warm regards and special thanks...

To my incredible mate, Laurie, and our four fantastic kids, Brooke, Heather, Collin and Brynne. You've been the most gracious to me when I was most absent from you. You're the best!

To my leaders and coworkers, Dutch, Bob, LeRoy, Dave, Jack, Brad, Gerri, Joy, Linda and Kay. I appreciate you.

To my church family at Springs Harvest Fellowship. What a wonderful group of people to "experiment" with in worship. I'm so grateful for your open hearts to the new things of God's Spirit.

To a host of prayer warriors and intercessors, Paula, Beth, Perry, Arlys, Barbara, Cindy, Sharon and Ann, who were always there to lift me up when the battle fatigue was most overwhelming. You guys are great!

To Cindy Jacobs for believing I had something to share and for placing your left foot squarely on my backside to get me motivated for this project.

To Ken, Randy, Alva and Jerry for creating time and space to chill out together. I appreciate the relationships and accountability we have shared.

To Mel for contributing to my creativity with your gift of a laptop computer.

To Jean for faithfully steering me down the road to healing.

To my editor, Karen Kaufman, for encouraging me to step into God's call for such a time as this. You've labored long and hard to make me sound good and keep me readable. I honor you and your gift of nurture to the Body of Christ. I'll never forget what you said on a few occasions: "An editor is like a doctor in the delivery room who says, 'It's a beautiful baby but it doesn't need this leg or that arm!'" Thank you for being so gracious in the delivery room and salvaging so much of my "child." You've been a marvelous midwife, knowing the exact time to yell, "PUSH!" And push, we did. Please accept the title of "godmother" to this book. You are a true newfound friend!

Chapter One

TAKING INVENTORY

Take my life and let it be,
Consecrated, Lord, to Thee;
Take my moments and my days.
Let them flow in ceaseless praise.

"TAKE MY LIFE AND LET IT BE"
BY FRANCIS R. HAVERGAL AND A. C. MALAN

The alarm rang! The clock read "5:30." I hit the snooze button. Nine minutes later, it rang again. The large glowing numerals on the dial now boasted "5:39." Again I hit the snooze button. This exhibition of personal discipline—or lack thereof—continued until 6:30 A.M. Now with hardly enough time for a quick shower and a cold bagel, I leaped out the door for another challenging day. If this particular morning had been the only one when I remained nearly comatose in my early morning, comfortably warm slumber, I would have rejoiced. Unfortunately, it was not! Day after day the routine continued with the same goal in mind: *I'm getting up early for devotions.*

I'd committed to spending some time alone with God before the day began. But it seemed that every time I tried to prove my love for Him by dragging my tired carcass out of bed early, I just could NOT rouse myself. This serious lack of personal spiritual discipline had become all too familiar. So familiar, in fact, that I could not summon the energy to change. Can you relate?

Slipping Through the Cracks on Greasy Grace!

I'd heard all my life about the importance of personal devotion and private worship. Desiring above all to gain points with God, I knew I must rise to this level of pristine performance if I were to get anywhere in the Kingdom. *After all, I thought, grace from God is only available after I've exhausted every other natural resource. I MUST prove my worth as a lover of God or He cannot help me. I must endeavor to prove that I am a man of God who is after His heart. I must prove... I must prove....*

A part of me wanted to bless the Lord with genuine love and faithfulness through this obedient act of a "quiet time." However, the proverbial "flesh and spirit" battle was raging within me. Oh, the war!!! I wondered, *Will there ever be a decisive victory in favor of the righteous side of me, or will I be held in the grips of this mediocre spiritual life forever?* With tenacity waning, I knew that somehow I had to stop and take some personal stock. I had to ask the hard questions: Why do I do what I do? and What's really inside of me, anyway?

Cleaning Out the Clutter

You know what it's like when you clean out the garage. You discover things that have been misplaced for years. Then again, you find things that should have been trashed long ago. The clutter often leaves you a bit perplexed as you think, *What in the world is THAT doing here? And what about those "spare* parts"? As a man, I can always find room for one more nut or bolt that has virtually NO significance! My thought is, *I may need that one day.* As slim as that truth may be, the fact remains that most of us tend to hold on to things much too long—even when their usefulness has been outlived by the need for more space.

If, indeed, we are not careful, we find that storage itself becomes the goal. We need more space for more stuff to satisfy the need for more ownership and control in our lives.

Our spiritual lives can also become warehouses for useless gratifying "stuff"—worldly attitudes, titles, past hurts, outdated traditions, old accomplishments and stale testimonies that do not reflect a "first love" for Jesus—thinking they will be useful down the road. But all they do is clutter up the garage, turning "storage" into a fiendish leech.

Our lives then tend to become compartmentalized. We develop containers for everything and call it organization, boundaries and discipline: This belongs to my occupational life; this belongs to my social life; this belongs to my family life; this belongs to my recreational life; this belongs to my spiritual life;...and the storage list continues.

Then Jesus comes along and says, "Can I look into that box?"

"THAT box, Lord?"

"Yes, that one—the one you have so carefully sealed, labeled and tucked away." Blushing, we try to negotiate a truce that will save us from the complete embarrassment of having Him prove to us that He really isn't Lord of that box. Any other box would be fine for Him to peruse....

The point is, He's trying to show us that our container system is useless to His all-seeing eye. Our "spiritual" boxes may be the biggest ones in storage, but they are still containers that can be opened and closed at our discretion and labeled "private." We pretend as though we can keep secrets from God, but in the depths of our hearts, we know there's nothing hidden from Him. Therefore, it's just a matter of time before He answers those prayers we've prayed for His lordship.

Playing the Part

My distorted and tainted views of Father God were based on years of practice. Therefore, I rehearsed ways in which I could please the God whom I believed to be an eternally angry Potentate. Though I was a Christian from an early age, I believed that perfection was the only acceptable offering. Proving myself and my love for God was based on nothing but what I thought I should DO for Him. Therefore my worship of Him was nothing but a "performance with a smile" on the stage of life. And if others were fooled into believing I was holy, then I, too, could believe I was.

Still, deep in my heart I knew there had to be more to this private life of devotion. I ached to know the God so many talked about on a deeply personal level. I longed to hear His voice and be comfortable alone with Him. I hungered for answers to the questions that plagued my mind: *Who is He really? What does He honestly require of me? How can I know Him in private devotion if I can't even get out of bed in the morning to seek Him? Why am I so afraid of Him?*

The problem resided in the fact that I did NOT know Him, nor did I trust Him. This wasn't God's fault, but rather a judgment I made about Him based on the way He had been portrayed to me throughout the years. I feared that His love was conditional and based upon my obedience to a rigid set of rules and regulations that paraded as "holiness." So the rules without the relationship produced rebellion, causing me to believe the lies propagated by the spirit of this world: *God is NOT friendly. God is angry at sin; therefore He's angry at you. You can never quite do enough to gain His favor. He is not knowable by the likes of you....*

Working for Love—Resisting Relationship

Worship from afar was the only answer. Maintaining distance from Him would keep me secure. My unconscious mind-set was: Just allow me enough of His presence to survive, but don't let Him get too close because He'll come in and wreck the sets on this beautiful stage I've built. I'll trust Him if I must, but only in the things I can't figure out for myself.

> *[Needing] approval from spiritual men...I gave them the authority to proclaim me righteous or unrighteous, justified or unjustified. This state of idolatry kept me marching to the drumbeat of man rather than resting in the heartbeat of God's love.*

What a grim existence! My faith was built on my ability to perform well for God. Doing and saying all the right things in the right ways was paramount to me; only the Lord knows how very hard I tried to comply. Be that as it may, the bottom line was that I had reduced my relationship with God to the need for approval from spiritual men. I gave them the authority to proclaim me righteous or unrighteous, justified or unjustified. This state of idolatry kept me marching to the drumbeat of man rather than resting in the heartbeat of God's love.

I cried out with the psalmist, "Teach me Thy way, O Lord; I will walk in Thy truth" (Ps. 86:11). I desperately needed an internal overhaul. Only God knew the honest depths of that cry more than I, but I was trapped! My so-called "knowledge of God" forbade me from coming closer to Him. My experience had dictated that He would not allow me to live my life. I feared losing that freedom. He would figuratively yet certainly kill me. Who I was would most certainly be offensive to Him. Truly in the light of His glorious holiness, I was lower than pond scum and could never expect to be accepted by Him.

I recognized my sinful nature and how large the chasm was between God and me. Even the blood of Jesus couldn't span that, I thought! The treadmill of performance was the only way to gain acceptance from God and access to His love. The guilt of sin was a factor but shame was the real culprit! I was ashamed of who I was. The person I had become with all my serious hidden faults was not acceptable to me, and I erroneously believed there was no way I could be acceptable to God—even through Jesus Christ.

Ending the Cycle of Performance and Shame

The cloud of shame that hovered over me robbed me of my sense of belonging, both to God and to the Body of Christ. It's strange how we can go through life with a full set of beautiful luggage filled with garbage and not even know it. Self-deception is rampant out there in people who believe they know and love God—honest people, for all practical purposes, but with blind eyes. The prophet Jeremiah showed his understanding of the inward parts of humanity when he wrote, "The heart is more deceitful than all else and is desperately sick; who can understand it?" (Jer. 17:9). Verily, who can understand the sickness in the heart of humankind but the Spirit of God who searches the hearts and knows them?

The gerbil's wheel I was on came to a screeching halt when I fell off, landing in immorality. It was a sick but relatively easy way to stop the cycle. The pattern of iniquity I had become so familiar with paved an enticing path to destruction. With my limited scope of God's love and the way I operated to please Him, it was only a matter of time before my energy level was depleted. I lost my proverbial footing, slipped and plunged headlong into the abyss of adultery.

Sometimes when we sin greatly, we are merely attempting to prove that we do not deserve God's love. We unwittingly believe that because we have been rejected and rejected ourselves, we can out-sin the magnitude of His incomprehensible compassion and love. And yet, it is only when we hit bottom that we find God's merciful arms stretched out to catch us.

As many who have fallen in this same destructive way have said to me, I never intended to hurt my wife, my children or the church family I belonged to. Despite my noble intentions, the choices I had made, based on my inability to maintain the pace I had set for myself, did a world of damage to many of those I loved and who loved me. The guilt was overwhelming. I couldn't bear to face ANYONE. There could be NO forgiveness and restoration for me. My sin was much greater than the love of God. The idol of self-sufficiency which I had worshiped for so long contributed to the length of time it took me to find God again.

Suicide became such a viable option that I soon believed there was no other choice. Fortunately, I had a major emotional collapse before I could do anything too damaging to myself or my family. I now see that experience as God's mercy upon me. Looking up through the bottom of life's darkest dungeon, I realized that if God didn't save me, I would never climb out of the hole I was in, and I would surely die!

Thus, I wrestled with myself and others' ideals of how to find God in the midst of this life-threatening situation. I still wince at times when I remember how frightened I was. I did not want to live without Jesus and His help. But I could not live with Him either, consistently faced with the reality of what I had done. I don't know if it's possible to describe the horror of a life hanging in the balance!

Even though I was medicated to correct a chemical imbalance, the depression was intense, with anger and fear plaguing me constantly. I ate damaging foods and introspected incessantly, all the while, mind you, searching for an answer to the gnawing question: How do I please a God who demands more than

I can give? I wanted out but there was no door. I needed relief but I found no remedy. I longed to sing again but the music in me had died. I ached to worship God but it seemed so hypocritical. I begged Him to either free me or kill me. There seemed to be no other way! Still the silence from heaven was deafening.

I wondered if the real me could ever experience the acceptance I so longed for. Would I ever be able to face people again? Would I ever be able to shamelessly worship the God I so longed to know? Then slowly...ever so slowly, the process of God's healing power began to peek over my dismal horizon as I daily chose to give up the ideas of who I thought God was. The aloneness I had experienced was the plan of God to reintroduce me to a brand-new concept of life called "Jesus."

A Look at the Real Me Through the Eyes of a Real Jesus

It took all the years of my growing up in the Church, through Bible School and into adulthood and ministry to come face-to-face with a holy God amid the shambles of my life. I had no "props" to support me or any trophies to justify my worth. There was no proving that I had done enough good to merit God's blessings upon me. There I stood, naked and alone before my Maker with nothing to offer Him but all my misunderstandings, bad attitudes and a lot of pain and fear. Then, with nothing but brokenness to offer and His mercy to appeal to, I heard Him say, "Ahh, now we can begin again." Instantly, the walls of my performance orientation began to crack. The light of His unconditional acceptance began to penetrate the darkness of shame's imprisoning walls. Through the literal valley of the shadow of death, I finally met the Lord—the REAL Jesus!

My "search for significance," as Robert McGee calls it, took me back to the roots of my Christian upbringing and the faith of my parents. As a believer in Jesus practically from birth, I was taught that everyone has a call from God and a destiny to fulfill. This idea, quite frankly, had been a nebulous concept until I reached an internal critical mass. Grappling with a number of decisions that would drastically change my future, I needed to rediscover myself in the light of an eternal perspective. I called my parents to discuss their conversion experience and the details surrounding my conception and birth. That February telephone conversation radically changed my philosophy of life and how I understood my call to ministry.

My parents shared how they had received the Lord in the early 1950s when the "Latter Rain" move of the Holy Spirit was at its peak. In the summer of 1958 while attending a prophetic meeting, the special speaker, who was a prophet, called them up to the front and began speaking prophetically into their lives. Among other things, he informed them that they would conceive yet another child. (At the time, they had four others at home and Mom didn't know she was expecting.) This child was called of God to bring glory to the Lord's name. The word "special" was used when referring to the gift God was about to deposit in their unborn baby. With gratefulness, my parents received that prophetic word from the Lord and hid it in their hearts until I was born.

When my parents first shared the words that had been spoken over me before my birth, I was completely taken aback by the plan of God for my life. I wept uncontrollably at the thought of the divine destiny that had been shaping me and was hidden from me, just out of reach, for most of my life.

Gifted and talented at an early age, I grew up on the piano bench and played in church from the age of five. It was easy to find my identity in my music because that's when I received the most recognition. I soon realized that I was "the entertainer" and keeping people happy was my number one job. I ultimately made myself responsible for everyone else's feelings. Regardless of a situation, I would walk into a room and find it my duty to provide happiness! Little did I know that I was assuming a pseudo-God role in many people's lives by allowing them to escape their reality through my talents. Eventually, the Lord would have to judge that performance, both for my sake and theirs.

I proceeded through life playing and singing, thinking, *That's who I am—I am what I do.* From time to time I would revolt against this pigeonhole I found myself in. I wanted to be treated like a person rather than a commodity, but the transition was too great. It was too difficult to try to create a new persona for presentation.

After talking with my parents, however, I now saw that even through the dark, painful difficulties of the seeming godlessness that had overtaken my soul, a thread of hope had been woven into the tapestry of my life, bringing a true revelation of His glorious calling. God did have a plan for me in spite of the enemy's designs to destroy the precious seed. And Jesus was literally redeeming my life from the pit, setting me free from the lies that defined me.

> *Because God had met me at the crash site, I now trusted Him to help me pick up the shattered pieces of my life and transform them into a tool for His glory and ministry to others.*

That day I began a journey which I intend to pursue as my life's goal: To consistently acknowledge my utter dependence upon God; to allow myself the luxury of this holy quest; to find His favor outside of my "perfect" performance; and to cultivate an awareness of Him through living life and giving myself to Him. The result? True worship!

True Worship: Knowing and Being Known by God

True worship flows out of freedom—the freedom to be real before God and, therefore, right with others. For me, that meant admitting my mistakes and humbling myself before my wife and friends. I had to fight my pride, my defensiveness and my desire to blame. I had broken their trust and left a lot of wreckage in my wake. But because God had met me at the crash site, I now trusted Him to help me pick up the shattered pieces of my life and transform them into a tool for His glory and ministry to others. And that is just what He has done. The result is a life that overflows with gratitude that I am forgiven. And such undeserved forgiveness is manifested in praise—a praise that is demonstrated in heartfelt worship.

As the years have passed, I've come to believe the responsibility that I assumed by confessing my sin to my wife and the church elders has produced an "on purpose" accountability that is now a comfort rather than a constraint. In submitting to an extended process of restoration, the Lord has truly restored me to my family and to the ministry that He called me to years ago. I've wrestled with sharing this part of my life, calculating the risk involved with this degree of transparency. As tenuous as my approach has been, I honestly believe my struggle is no more unique than that of the many others who don't feel the freedom to share their pain or their triumph over such sin.

Though your experience may not be as obvious or dramatic in realizing God's foreordained call, the fact remains according to His Word that He has predestined each of us—that includes "you," no matter how shattered your life may be—to be conformed to the image of His Son (see Rom. 8:29). His divine intention for all humanity is that we come to know Him and be known by Him through an encounter with His love. The primary source for this experience is worship—a worship that pours out of genuine love and gratitude to God.

The pain of years gone by has been removed, but the scars remain to remind me of how God's kindness led me to repentance. The memories are the consequences of sin, but God's grace and mercy become evident as memories give way to gratefulness. Hindsight is 20/20. It's so difficult to see clearly through eyes of faith when you're in the middle of your darkest hour. We desperately need someone to walk through it with us. Even Jesus longed for the fellowship of others in the garden of Gethsemane (see Mark 14:32-41). I thank God for the special friends who kept me from jumping off the bridge on more than one occasion.

Just as God did not leave me comfortless, He is there to comfort you as well. The Scripture says that He is a friend who sticks closer than a brother (see Prov. 18:24), and He has promised never to leave you or forsake you (see Deut. 31:8; Heb. 13:5).

For those of you who may be dealing with a sensitive moral situation that has or is in the process of destroying your life and relationships, there is hope in a God who knows your depths and is familiar with your humanity. Please allow me to lead you in a prayer:

Father, often the thing that keeps me from total transparency is fear of exposure. I feel as though I'm the only one who can protect myself and my family from the serious repercussions of my poor choices. If people knew what was going on with me, they might reject me, and their possible rejection of me is too painful to risk. I know I must trust You in any process of repentance, restoration and restitution. I ask for Your great mercy to flood my mind and deliver me from self-destructive thinking. I choose to trust You at this juncture in life regardless of what others may think. I desire holiness over convenience and Your favor above all else. Oh, Great Physician, as I repent of my idolatry, pour Your healing ointment over my brokenness and bind the wound that keeps me from You. In Jesus name. Amen.

Now trust God to answer that prayer. He is for you, not against you. I am living proof that God is still in the business of restoring the brokenhearted. Today, the future is bright. Not because I've reached a perfected stage of spirituality by any means, but because each day is now recognized as a gift from God. And because I have visited a personal hell already, tomorrow can only be better! Today I say, "This is the day that the Lord has made. I will rejoice and be glad in it!" Today I want to live and be free to love Him potentially more than yesterday. The pathway of learning that nothing can separate me from the love of God in Christ Jesus has been paved with pain, but it has taken me to a place of grace—the Promised Land—where life is no longer dependent on my performance but His undeserved forgiveness and favor. I now live and breathe and find my life in Him.

My Wholehearted Pursuit

In my Bible School days, each year Joy Dawson was invited as a guest lecturer. Her dynamic teaching on the fear of the Lord always evoked a fresh commitment to holiness from the student body. I'll never forget those penetrating words that sparked holy fervor in me: "God rewards the diligent seeker, not just the casual inquirer."

It took several years of healing for me to see, believe and practice the principles of asking, seeking and knocking (see Matt. 7:7; Luke 11:9). The consistency of building my faith in a God whom I'd seen as distant and uncaring about details was painfully grueling at times. The choice to trust in Him was a daily exercise of humility. What I found in this holy pursuit for the diligent seeker was the answer of God when the "fullness of time" had come —when the Lord knew I was best equipped to sustain all the repercussions of the change I prayed for, and when I could best walk in the truth He would bring.

The ongoing, progressive revelation of God as my loving heavenly Father and His truth caused me to finally find Him and the answers I had searched for all of my life. I finally realized the truth that "the one who has entered His rest has himself also rested from his works" (Heb. 4:10). A lifestyle that is pleasing to God is one that finds its rest in Him so that He can do His work in us and eventually through us. Someone has said that we must constantly beware that the work we are doing for God does not interfere with the work He is doing in us.

Truth: The Foundation for Intimacy

For some, the truth may come in times of refreshing and renewal of vision and fervor toward God. For others, it may come slower and through more traumatic events that reduce them to emotional ruin and rubble. A day-by-day walk toward some uncharted goal can create a tedious and pessimistic view of God's ways, thinking, *He must be punishing me for something, otherwise He would have shown up already.* As real as those feelings are, the Scripture says, "The Lord is near to the broken-hearted, and saves those who are crushed in spirit" (Ps. 34:18).

Too often we are oblivious to the Lord's delivering hand in the midst of the darkness. We cry out, "Where are You, God?????" when all the while, He is standing right next to us. Our expectations of Him commonly surpass our faith. I expected the Lord to just "show up" and save me out of my despair without having to exercise my faith and genuine trust in Him. His plan, however, was to bring me to a place where I would choose to believe His character based on the truth revealed in His Word rather than how I felt. He was teaching me to trust what I could not see—the art of peacefully abiding in Him though all around was a raging storm of emotional turmoil. Through a process called "LIFE," I discovered that the art of abiding in Him is cultivated, watered, cared for, nourished and nurtured.

Back to the Garden

I don't think it's any mistake that man's existence began in a garden. The Bible says man is created from the earth. So caring for the earth can be a way of nurturing our own souls. For me, vegetable gardening has been a therapeutic passion. I launched into it as a recovery technique years ago. I'm fascinated by both the simplicity and genetic complexities of life found in the smallest seed. I find it hard to fathom that nourishing food comes out of the ground.

I've discovered that preparation is the first key to a healthy garden. Throughout the year I keep a compost pile, adding grass clippings and biodegradable kitchen scraps. Maintaining that mix properly is a challenge all its own. When the winter months pass, I till the fallow soil, mixing in the compost and fertilizer. Then, when the danger of frost is gone, the fun part begins as the seeds are planted in their assigned rows and spaces.

I enjoy measuring the distance that each vegetable needs for proper growth. For example, zucchini and pumpkins need more space than lettuce and carrots. Space and time are important when plotting out the format of the garden. After the planting there is more work to pursue...watering, weeding, watching and WAITING!

Patience is said to be a virtue, which must mean it is a quality worth investing in. I've found that gardening can bring out the best and worst in a person's patience level. Some plants are "late" bloomers. The seed packet says to allow 21 days for germination. But what do you do when 24 days later, there's still nothing green popping up? Do you succumb to the temptation to dig up that little sprout to see what's going on? Do you abandon the entire agricultural process out of frustration and delay? NO WAY!!! You exercise patience and wait another day or two...or three...or four....Unless there is something innately incompatible with the soil or the weather, sooner or later those seedlings turn into real live plants!

I had been faithful to till the soil, fertilize, plant, water, watch and wait! But I had to continue to believe that what I had sown would bear fruit. Some days after watering, all I could do was sit and watch with great anticipation. And pray...and pray...and pray. Every morning and every night in the garden I would ask, "Lord, please bless the work of my hands. Prosper these few crops and let them be a blessing to my family."

Cultivating a Lifestyle of Worship

Don't you just love that feeling of accomplishment when all your hard work finally pays off and you can sit back and enjoy the fruit of your labor? My time with God in private devotion and worship became very much the same as tending the garden. It took a serious investment of time and energy before the Lord brought permanent change to my life through personal times of devotion. It became evident to me that just as certain seeds need more time than others to germinate, God's truths have germination times as well. Some truths of God and His character are more easily assimilated than others. Just when I thought I had it figured out, more time was necessary for the deeper truths because of their root systems.

I begged Him for the miraculous "ZAP" that would turn me into the holy, righteous and godly person I desired to be. I asked Him repeatedly to "grow me up" in a hurry, but He didn't work like that. He used the process of time-developed relationship and my gardening experiences to show me that His principles of sowing and reaping are both natural and spiritual laws. I learned that lasting changes happen over life, not over night. We don't get a life—we cultivate a life. It must cost us something because we must invest in the land to fully appreciate it. Financial investments, job seniority, child rearing and education all fall into this same category. Paying the price includes time, energy and money!

Likewise, there is a cost to the pursuit of holiness that most are unaware of or perhaps unwilling to pay. And many who are willing are looking for the bargain rate. The price of holiness, however, never goes on sale! Those can be difficult words to hear. And we who have invested time and energy walking out of a performance-based relationship with God often find it hard to know what to do with the idea of investing in godliness without stepping right back onto "the stage."

Our challenge is to establish the fact in our hearts that the *love* of God is forever secured and cannot be earned or shaken.

But the *blessings* of God are contingent upon our obedience. If the Lord says, "Seek My face," our response must be, "Your face, Lord, I will seek!"

Worship: A Heart for God

I'm reminded of King David's plan to build an altar to the Lord on the threshing floor. The property was being given to David by the owner, but David would not accept it. He said, "No, but I will surely buy it from you for a price, for I will not offer burnt offerings to the Lord my God which cost me nothing" (2 Sam. 24:24). It would seem that David understood the need to "pursue" God by making his search valuable and calculated. It wasn't a happenstance or coincidental occurrence that David stumbled onto. He set his heart to love the Lord by an act of his will, regardless of his life's often difficult situations. He chose to put a priority on his pursuit of God. And oh, how God liked that about David—even in spite of his faults and blatant sin.

There was something uniquely special about David's ability to express himself. What was it that enabled him to freely and emotionally articulate his praise and worship as well as his pain and fears to God? Could it be the simplicity of an open heart before Him? Perhaps it was that there was no guile or deceit in David's heart. It seems that he didn't need to prove anything to himself or to others. David did not live for the praise of people; he lived for openness with God. He refused to hide his humanity from God by wrapping himself in a religious cloak. He was a real person with real feelings and was unashamed of celebrating life—even if he didn't always respond perfectly to life's situations.

David characterizes for most of us what a godly man is truly like: Strong masculinity combined with deep sensitivity and creativity that erupts in heartfelt passion toward God. His is the kind of soul that shouts, "I was created for THIS: to love God with all of my being!" This is the kind of abandon God is looking for.

I can almost hear you saying, "I want a heart like David's...one after God's own heart! But my personality won't permit me to be so emotional...I'm not like that. I tend to be more reserved and in control of my feelings. Can I still have that kind of relationship without all the hoopla?" The answer is YES! when you allow the God who created you to be your Master...which means that what He desires is what gives you the greatest pleasure. I've heard it expressed in the following words:

> There are two great passions in the universe: God's passion to be glorified and man's passion to be satisfied. However, these two do not need to conflict. They can come to simultaneous fulfillment in worship, because God is most glorified in me when I am most satisfied in Him alone.[1]

It's time to discard all the containers...to open all your sealed boxes. Let Him know you "warts and all." You cannot shock Him. He sees and knows more about you than you know about yourself. Get to know Him through His Word. Let the depths of His character touch the roots of your being. Let His unconditional love uproot your shame until your heart is over-whelmed with gratitude—then all that you do will become an act of worship and your life will become a song of praise.

Note

1. Tom Kraeuter, *Worship Is...What?!* (Lynnwood, Wash.: Emerald Books, 1996), p. 14.

IN HOT PURSUIT

Day by day and with each passing moment,
Strength I find to meet my trials here;
Trusting in my Father's wise bestowment,
I've no cause for worry or for fear.
He whose heart is kind beyond all measure
Gives unto each day what He deems best;
Lovingly, it's part of pain and pleasure,
Mingling toil with peace and rest.

"DAY BY DAY"
BY CAROLINA SANDELL BERG AND OSCAR AHNFELT

So, what about daily devotions? Unfortunately for many of us, they have been neither daily nor devotional—and there are a million reasons why! Perhaps we've looked at them as a chore, a discipline or a test from God. In any case, for most of us daily devotions have at one time or another been less than convenient—and sometimes even stressful. Adding one more thing to an already overcrowded schedule creates more unrest. If only we could be assured that the time we invest will be greatly worth our while. Carefully we whisper to ourselves, *Besides fighting guilt and keeping God happy, what will this do for ME?*

Chapter Two

It's a Question of Ownership

First, we must understand that personal worship and private devotion are based on ownership. Let me ask you a few questions: To whom do you belong? In the compartmentalization of your busy life, where is the greatest amount of your affection invested? Is Jesus your Lord and Master, or is He an additive to your weekend life like golf is to a busy week? Do you allow Him to speak to you at any moment of the day, or must He make an appointment? Does He have permission to rearrange your time as He chooses, or must He sit through a negotiation procedure? (I get a little nervous when people talk about arguing with God. Who do you think will win?)

If the earth is the Lord's and everything in it, that means I belong to Him as well. That's why He is "a jealous God." I'm His and that's it! My choice as to how I respond to His ownership can bring either joy or sorrow to my life. The real question is not, How much of *my* time will I give to Him? No, the real question is, How much of the time He has given me is under His lordship?

In our western culture, independence and arrogant self-centeredness have embraced the late Frank Sinatra's "My Way" as a theme song. Independence from anything that hints of improper control is quintessential to our comfortable existence, which is partly God-given in His "free will" package to humanity. However, in its inflated humanistic stage, it shakes a fist in God's face and says, "Who do You think You are? I'm in charge of my own life."

At some point we must come face-to-face with God's ownership. It's really the only way we can truly receive His love. If we can embrace the fact that the blood of Jesus *purchased* us for God, we will find greater peace in knowing He has our lives in His hands. If He owns us by way of a legal purchase agreement, then He must have a vested interest in His possession. After trying to govern my own life and failing miserably, it's a warm comfort to trust in Someone bigger than I!

The faith factor comes in *trusting* the God who made me, redeemed me and destined me for sonship from the beginning of time. If what He did on the Cross was just for me (which it was), then His pursuit of me was not finished when He died. He knows I desperately need help applying the power of the Cross to my daily life. My responsibility is to say yes to Him. His responsibility is to do the necessary work: "For it is God who is at work in [me], both to will and to work for His good pleasure" (Phil. 2:13).

He draws me to Himself and I respond by following. Yes, I make the choice to be led like a sheep, but He does the leading like a shepherd. He pursued me first, whether I see that or not. He didn't wait for me to beg for mercy but He died for me before I knew I needed Him. What an incredible love! With a working revelation of His pursuit of me, I find the often hidden desire rising to the surface that must give way to reciprocate the pursuit.

It's as simple as seeing Him show up in an otherwise ordinary day. As you become aware of His presence, it suddenly *dawns* on you—God is here, and you respond, "Oh Lord, I'm once again overwhelmed by Your obvious love for me. My heart cries out....How I love You, Jesus." The pursuit becomes a two-way street, bringing completion to the circle of the relationship. Oh, if only it were like that always...for everyone....

A Heavenly Courtship

Relationships, however, don't just happen; they require an investment of quality time, getting to know each other. Have you ever been in love? Remember those days and the precious time "devoted" to the relationship? Remember how you couldn't wait to be together again? What were the qualities of that relationship that pressed you into a mode of pursuit? Was it an emotional bond or an identification with a mutual concern? Could it have been a physical attraction? Was it the ideal of what you wanted to be that you saw mirrored in that person? What about the mutuality of the pursuit? Was the relationship founded on a one-sided ideal?

Imagine with me for a moment...a young man sees a lovely

young woman across the room at a party. Instantly his heart says he must meet her. Desiring to pursue her, he awkwardly approaches and asks for her phone number—all the while knowing he faces the risk of rejection. Then to his surprise, she offers her number with a smile.

Overjoyed at this new prospect, the young man makes immediate plans to set up a date. Being the proper fellow that he is, he arrives at the girl's home and asks to speak with her father. The father, of course, invites him in and they share brief pleasantries. After confidence is re-awakened, the young man asks her father if he may spend some time with his daughter. Pleased by the manners of this guy, the father grants permission.

Standing in the parlor, waiting for the moment when she descends the stairs, the young man is filled with anticipation. He waits...and waits....Finally, the housekeeper comes down the stairs with a note from the girl. It reads, "How nice of you to come this evening. I'm delighted that you want to be with me. Perhaps you could leave a picture of yourself with a note for me on the bureau in the hall before you go. Personal interaction is a bit much for me; therefore, I would be more comfortable if we could correspond this way."

Stunned, the young man slowly walks out the door, rethinking his pursuit of such an eccentric girl. *Why would she treat me so?* he thinks. *Why would she let me believe there was a potential future in this relationship and then hide upstairs in her bedroom? Was she just leading me on? Is she afraid of me?...Perhaps she's changed her mind and doesn't want a relationship. Maybe I did something wrong....*

These, along with a host of other thoughts, go through the guy's head as he tries to understand what has just happened. The feelings of rejection and embarrassment are almost paralyzing. Now what? Should he continue to pursue the girl or forget her and go on to another? What would you do?

OK, now relate this scenario to the Lord's pursuit of you and me. Can you hear the cry of the Bridegroom for His Bride? He longs to not only send a *"Letter"* to those of us He calls His Bride but to also spend quality time with us. He is committed to the relationship; therefore, His love never fails. He never gives up in spite of our "too busy" and often fearful lives. So how do you think Jesus feels when we show a distancing kind of attitude toward Him?

> *Oh, if only we could see and receive the pursuit of His heart of love for us...we could cease our striving to be so "perfect."*

He's in hot pursuit of those who desire to receive His love. I think all of us would concur that we want to receive it, but for many it's easier to talk about than to actually receive.

A lot of people call themselves "Christians" but few are truly "Christlike." Similarly, a bunch of people worship on weekends but not enough are true *worshipers.* I believe this discrepancy is evidence that many people don't really know Him. Could it be that millions of Christians have a similar history to mine and only know God in ways that keep them running a futile race of performance for Him? Oh, if only we could see and receive the pursuit of His heart of love for us...we could cease our striving to be so "perfect."

A Lifestyle of Worship Means Ongoing Repentance

He alone is perfect and we enter into His perfect will for our lives through repentance—an acknowledgment of the lack of genuine desire for God, yet a willingness to be changed by His loving embrace. This doesn't have to be monumental. The word "repentance" may cause you to think, *Oh great, just one more thing to repent of....Maybe one day I'll arrive.* Most of us have been there. We tend to feel, *If only I could get past this "initial step" of repentance and get on with the rest of life.* However, repentance is a lifestyle, which is why Scripture tells you and me to "work out your salvation" (Phil. 2:12).

I'm convinced the *process* of changing our minds and hearts to be like Jesus will take the rest of our lives, giving us more time to better know Him in the power of His resurrection and the fellowship of His sufferings. Let the repentance begin so we can know Him! Will you pray this prayer of repentance with me now:

Father,
Thank you for unveiling the truth of Your unfailing love and Your desire toward me. Please forgive me for allowing "things" to consume my time and energy, robbing me of genuine desire for You and Your ways. Help my unbelief and transform it into a firm faith in Your ways. Help my unbelief and transform it into a firm faith in Your consistent care for me. Help me understand that knowing You IS eternal life and that I can partake of life NOW!

Worship Is a Choice

Everything we succeed at in life begins with our choices. As we simply choose to show up for devotions, God will meet us there. Then as we spend time in His presence, He will answer the longings of our hearts. These times can transform us into *worshipers* of God rather than *visitors* of God. Do remember, He's interested in a Bride; not a weekend girlfriend!

In the famous worship passage of John 4 when Jesus addresses the woman at the well, verse 23 reads: "The time...is here when the true (genuine) worshipers will worship the Father in spirit and in truth (reality), for the Father is seeking just such people as these as His worshipers" (*Amp.*). It becomes evident that the revelation Jesus states in this passage is nothing less than heretical to this lady looking for living water. She immediately refers to Him as a prophet.

The argument for centuries between the Jews and Samaritans up to this point had been, On which mountain are we to worship? Apparently the concept of *worship* had been reduced to a stated time and place at a temple on one of two mountains in Palestine: Mount Moriah or Mount Gerrizim. This idea holds some familiarity to our present culture with most believers looking at worship as an activity that takes place only on Sundays at 10:00 A.M.!

For this woman, who may represent the desire of all religious experiences gone awry, it's obvious Jesus was trying to draw an enormous distinction between *worship* and *worshipers*. If we could grasp this fact in its purest form, we would be much more fulfilled in our daily walk with the Father, realizing that He wants to *know* us through relationship rather than just *visit* with us on occasion. God is looking for *worshipers* rather than for *worship*.

The Worshiper

A worshiper is one who allows the Holy Spirit to transform his or her heart and life through an act of worship, turning worship into more than just a religious activity. A worshiper knows that the activity of worship is merely an avenue for expressing his or her basic disposition toward God. The worshiper's general view of life could be stated: "My life belongs to God and what I *do* in worship to God is a reflection of *who I am*, but more importantly, *whose I am*."

In the apostle Paul's second letter to the church at Corinth, Paul shares his concern: "But I am afraid, lest as the serpent deceived Eve by his craftiness, your minds should be led astray from the simplicity and purity of devotion to Christ" (2 Cor. 11:3). In contemporary words, *complication hinders communion!* Whatever happened to, "Jesus loves me, this I know; for the Bible tells me so"? Can it get any simpler than this—or should we say, must it be any more complicated than this?

Oh, the simplicity of pure devotion to Christ! The primary element here is "devotion to Christ," and we must make that as simple as possible. From the depths of our souls comes a cry to know God simply, truly and deeply without all the trappings and extra baggage that religious endeavors tend to place on us. In our hearts we want to run away from all the formulas that have exhausted us through the years in our attempts to be spiritually acceptable to God, hoping He will accept the sacrifice of our time and energy as an offering. Think about it...What is He after really? Not all our efforts—but us—a relaxed and honest YOU and ME! If He knows me inside and out, then why should I try to be something other than me?

With all the devotional tools available—prayer journals, devotional books and specialized Bibles for men, women and children, Scripture memory aids, daily workbooks of all sorts—one would think that Christendom has mastered the art of the pursuit of God...only to find that there is one more book out there yet to be written on the subject. By all means take advantage of these aids, and use whatever it takes to achieve the goal of gaining wisdom, but keep in mind that the true change in us comes from knowing the Lord personally...intimately. Pure and simple devotion to MY God because He's touched MY life!

Worship Is an Intimate Encounter with God

The word "intimacy" conjures up a plethora of definitions for both men and women. Women tend to appreciate the idea as important to deep relationship. Conversely, many men tense up at the very mention of the word. Why is this so? What are the fears associated with intimacy and the masculine image? Fear of being uncovered...fear of being known...fear of showing "weakness" or need...fear of honesty...fear of rejection...and the list continues.

In every case, thanks be to God, healing is available for those fears that stifle the presence of God we earnestly need for wholeness. This process usually includes forgiveness of parents, siblings and friends for things they don't even know they've done that damaged our ability to trust. As the Lord is allowed to touch that pain and heal the wound, trust in Him can be reestablished. Ask the Lord to expose any hidden hurts in you that you have been afraid to look at. Then ask Him to help you grieve the loss or the pain and picture yourself giving the situation up to Him. God is faithful.

Healing is an ongoing process. I personally watch for areas where I still have hurts. Every six months or so, I like to get away by myself for a few days for a private retreat. I've received much healing from the Lord during those times as fears surface and become obvious. Graciously, Jesus shows up to dismantle a belief system that is like a weed—when left alone, it grows like wild! I also see the importance of those times as an opportunity for *decongesting*. Life is filled with so many things to do that too often God gets lost in the stacks of my chores. I learned to do this by studying the life of Jesus, who pulled away for private communion with the Father on a regular basis.

In times of reflection I often see an intense preoccupation in my life with the work of the ministry. I'm so encumbered with things to do for God that I easily lose sight of *HIM*, the object of my worship. Sometimes it takes as many as three days to fully unload my soul before I can receive an impartation of something fresh from the Lord. It's during those times that I feel His gentle tug on me to return to simplicity.

On the back cover of Henri Nouwen's book, *The Way of the Heart*—in which he encapsulates a lifestyle of worship and private devotion, focusing on solitude, silence and prayer—Madeline L'Engle writes:

In these increasingly more sound-polluted and frenetic years, Henri Nouwen's simple words about the prayer of the heart will be helpful for all who seek to turn from the complex wiles of the world to the simplicity of the love of God.[1]

The ongoing lesson learned is that proper maintenance of God's life in me is absolutely essential for the "rivers of living water" to flow and not stagnate. The challenge is daily availability! I must "allow" the rivers to flow by creating times to commune with the Lord. There must be interludes in my life where I just *"waste"* time on the Lord.

"Wasting" Time on the Time Giver

When a person's life is taken, his or her time is gone. Time is life. It is our most precious commodity! You hear it all day long from coworkers, friends, family members—even your spouse: "I don't have time!" What is it that consumes so much of this expensive resource? Am I living to build my kingdom or His? Have I succumbed to the worship of the clock rather than the God who created it? How can I "redeem" this God-ordained method of limitation?

Much of what we do with time is a matter of habit. And implementing new habits will require a plan and some pain. If we are in the "swing" of a regular schedule that does *not* include a quality date with God, the chore of rearranging can be energy depleting and take more *time*—especially for those of us who tend to be unmotivated to change our perfectly laid out plans. But we can change and that is where we must place our focus.

As difficult as our schedules may be to reconcile, consider God's call to holiness upon our lives and hear the lyrics of this poignant nineteenth-century hymn:

Take *time* to be holy, speak oft with thy Lord;
Abide in Him always, and feed on His Word,
Make friends of God's children, help those who are weak;
Forgetting in nothing His blessing to seek.
Take *time* to be holy, the world rushes on;

Spend much *time* in secret with Jesus alone.
By looking to Jesus like Him thou shalt be;
Thy friends in thy conduct His likeness shall see.
      by William D. Longstaff and George C. Stebbins

By *"wasting"* time on God, I avail myself to partake of His divine, holy nature. I can literally take on His characteristics by being with Him and allowing Him to saturate my life with His presence in the quiet place of personal devotion. For it is not what I receive from my time alone with God but who I become that is the real miracle.

In the book *A God Who Heals the Heart*, Steve Fry recites:

Holiness is indeed the response to privilege, not the summons to performance. Holiness is living out our cho-senness; it is apprehending our status."[2]

We've sung the old song, "To be like Jesus, to be like Jesus. All I ask is to be like Him." But how does that happen? Change happens as we spend time with the Creator. It is what Steve Fry refers to as "apprehending our status"—an active pursuit in waiting on God. God is looking for a heart that desires to pursue Him so He can pour in His holiness. He is searching for a heart that is open to hear His voice.

And yet if it's possible to speak to Him and listen to Him for an hour or more, why do I groan at the thought? Probably because I have so many other things to do and my ability to budget my time is still lacking in maturity. I let the "other things" rule my clock and not the wooing and pursuing of God's Spirit.

True Worship: Sitting at His Feet

In Luke chapter 10 (the second most popular passage for teaching on worship in the Bible), it's interesting to observe Mary and Martha's responses during Jesus' visit. As Jesus is speaking with Mary in the living room, Martha is fretting in the kitchen. The poor dear is frustrated that she's having to do all the work while Mary is "kicking back," visiting with the Master Teacher.

Although some words are exchanged, it's difficult for me to believe that Jesus would actually criticize Martha for functioning in her role as a firstborn, duty-bound, practical-arrangement-oriented individual. I believe He was really trying to divert her attention to the eternal significance that was present in her home. Yes, supper preparation was on the list as was cleaning the house and arranging for the guests. However, Martha had not quite grasped that history was in the making as the Son of God was imparting words of life to her little sister.

Jesus simply makes a statement to Martha: "Martha, dear Martha, you're fussing far too much and getting yourself worked up over nothing. One thing only is essential, and Mary has chosen it—it's the main course, and won't be taken from her" (Luke 10:41,42, *The Message*).

Recently my pastor, Dutch Sheets, spoke of this scenario in a sermon:

> Martha was distracted by her ministry to and for Jesus in the kitchen. The Greek word for "distracted" here has the firm implication that one drags his or her ministry around in circles. It was as if Mary should say to Martha, "Well, if He wants something to eat, He'll have to quit talking—cause I'm doing nothing until He stops."[3]

Have you ever been so "caught up" in doing good deeds for God that the life which the work used to bring to you has ebbed away and now all you're able to do is drag it around in circles...distracted from the goal of pure devotion? If so, it's time to make a change in your ministry philosophy!

In the context of personal worship and private devotion, I think Jesus would like us to understand that the legitimate cares and concerns of life are not evil and will still be there *after* our time alone with Him. The choice is not either/or, but rather a time-management issue based on priority. As it was with Mary and Martha when Jesus was present, Mary chose the *good* part in that her choice of timing was good. It was time to listen to Jesus at that moment, not fix supper or clean the house.

Of the several times Mary is mentioned in the New Testament, most are in the context of her giving something of value or worship to the Lord. Her alabaster box filled with the costly ointment spikenard from India is just one example of the worth she placed on Jesus as she *"wasted"* her most precious possession on the Master.

When I have a scheduled date with God, my confidence is in knowing that Jesus is delighted to be there to impart words of life. I encourage myself with the thought, *He pursued me first and gave everything He had to provide this awesome relationship with the Father of Life!* If He sacrificed everything to give me life, then I can simply show my appreciation by creating time to share intimate moments during our quiet time. So I pray, "Lord, grant me the sense to choose the good part and show up to open the alabaster box of my heart!"

Do I ever miss my appointments with God? Sure I do! But I'm much more aware now of His gentle voice calling me to be with Him rather than hearing how horrible I am for failing to make our date. My relationship with God reflects a sense of freedom as do all good friendships.

Friendship Takes Two

Friendships that last have one common ingredient: effective communication. This is also true of our relationship with God. If we are to gain the depth in God we long for, not only do we need to give Him the praise He deserves, but we also need to receive His embrace as a loving Father. Our worship must be interwoven with both giving and receiving.

Monologue is an activity performed by one person. I can talk to God all day long and only accomplish half the goal. But dialogue is the exchange between two parties where ideas and thoughts are mutually shared. Worship is the highest level of communication between God and man. As He reveals a portion of His character, I respond in praise to His glorious light. Overjoyed at my response, He then shows me another facet of Himself to which I respond with another acclamation of worship. This divine communication between us fulfills His original desire with Adam in the garden...to walk together sharing thoughts, ideas and emotions.

Some days in private worship I say very little. I just feel like being still with God and letting Him speak to me. Other days, I need to tell Him everything that is on my heart. As in every close friendship, sometimes you just need your friend to listen to you share your joys and fears. You're not expecting that person to really respond to you—just to listen. Then there are those days when mutual conversation is vital. Those times with the Lord are special as He imparts sound counsel in the midst of a potentially disturbing situation.

Worship and the Word

His written Word is one of our greatest tools for instruction and revelation. Have you ever just sat and opened the Bible in a moment of quiet trust (or even frenzied, wild-eyed frustration) and watched the Lord unfold something so simple yet profound? How awesome to posture yourself before the Almighty God with His Word until some particular passage becomes supernaturally activated enough to change the direction of your day—and ultimately your life! You sit there with your mouth open and say, "WOW, I've never seen that before. Hard to believe *that* has been in the Bible all these years." That's the power of His ingested Word.

When the light shines on the Scriptures, I find myself giving thanks to God for the power of the Word and worshiping Him as the God who knows me so deeply that He put that particular verse in there just for me—today. It opens up a whole new world of thanksgiving, releasing an eternal perspective on my short, vaporous life.

When the light comes silently and moves me to contemplation and meditation, I become gratefully introspective, realizing the God of the universe is speaking to *me*. When I ingest it audibly, I am moved to act on this fresh revelation as faith comes by *hearing* the Word. Change then becomes inevitable when the Word is conceived in my heart!

There's something about reading the Word aloud that changes the atmosphere around you and actually produces faith! Sadly enough though, being verbal about the promises of God often kicks against the concrete walls of our comfort zones. We say, "God knows my heart, I don't need to be so verbal." True...only God knows the heart—the enemy does NOT! (See Ps. 94:11; Heb. 4:12.) He cannot read our minds or the intents of our hearts. That is why we must declare aloud God's promises, provisions and His salvation: "Let the redeemed of the Lord *say so*" (Ps. 107:2, italics added). It is crucial to exercise our wills to choose faith in God by speaking His Word. And as we speak His Word, our faith begins to grow, causing us to trust God more and more.

Worship: A Love Song

Along the same line, I also find it essential to sing songs of adoration to God in private worship. Mainly because I've never liked to listen to myself sing. However, when I do so in private, I'm forced to hear myself honor God with the voice He gave me—it's great for extinguishing my pride! After the first song or so, I'm able to shift my attention from me to Him. Often enough I find myself speaking and singing the Psalms and other Scriptures aloud just to rouse my attention to the living Word. The "by-product" is the aesthetic impact I "feel" in the release of my soul as it is expressed to God. To sing is to allow the creative juice of God to flow through me.

"But what if I can't sing?" Please understand that singing is NOT worship. It is a vehicle whereby we express worship. My opinion, though, is that everyone can sing to some degree unless a physical impairment is present. The way God created our vocal chords to sustain pitch and tone is proof enough. Unfortunately, many of us have listened to others tell us we *can't* sing or do it so poorly that we've adopted a scoffer's view of the Scripture that exhorts us to "sing to Him a new song" (Ps. 33:3). Your performance is not the issue; your heart is the issue.

> *"The condition to receiving God's full blessing is absolute surrender to Him."*
> *—Andrew Murray*

The Creator of the very gift you bring to Him is delighted at any joyful noise that is humbly offered! Freewill "offering" is the operative word in worship.

Surrendering Self

The most fundamental point of personal devotion and private worship takes into account the whole of life. It's probably the simplest of concepts but the one most overlooked when we talk about worship. Andrew Murray once stated, "The condition to receiving God's full blessing is absolute surrender to Him."[4]

The apostle Paul speaks of submitting ourselves to God in all things. He addresses the church at Ephesus and Colossae with similar instruction regarding family and work-related ethical conduct. He encourages both churches to include the use of psalms, hymns and spiritual songs in corporate worship (see Eph. 5:19; Col. 3:16).

He then admonishes husbands to love their wives, wives to submit to their husbands, children to obey parents and employees to submit to employers..."not by way of eyeservice, as men-pleasers, but as slaves of Christ, doing the will of God from the heart" (Eph. 6:6). "And whatever you do in word or deed, do all in the name of the Lord Jesus, giving thanks through Him to God the Father....Whatever you do, do your work heartily, as for the Lord rather than for men....It is the Lord Christ whom you serve" (Col. 3:17,23,24).

True worship of God is broadened to the extreme boundaries of personal, family, church, occupational and social arenas. God is to be honored on every level of life so His children don't become hypocrites—given to a practice of consecration only on Sundays at 10:00 A.M., while behaving like those who have no knowledge of Him the rest of the week.

If I am unable to "sanctify" or separate myself unto God daily as a worship offering, then do I really have any business going to the house of God on Sunday to sing songs of the faith that I can't live by on the other six days of the week? Shall I declare the lordship of Jesus in the congregation and neglect His rule at home or on the job?

When Jesus is truly confessed as Lord of our lives, challenges become opportunities to extend the borders of His dominion and defeat the enemy all at once.

Sunday's worship time is no more an act of worship than is being a loving husband, wife or parent, practicing hospitality, being active in worthy community efforts or doing our jobs wholeheartedly. True worship is submitting my body to God as a living and holy sacrifice, acceptable to Him, which is my "spiritual service of worship" (Rom. 12:1). A true worshiper is one who sees the Lord daily in private and through life's mundane activities while maintaining a Kingdom perspective and heart condition. The result being the declaration that, "I can do this as unto the Lord, bringing glory to Him because He genuinely delights in me. I am a worshiper of the living God, a vessel of honor that is fit for the Master's use. My life is not my own; it is His."

I not only confess that I am a worshiper of God with my mouth, but I must also demonstrate that fact by keeping my appointments with Him, loving my wife, caring for my children, working heartily in the garden and giving my best to my employer. Jesus is the one whom I serve—not men. Therefore, all that I do can be done in the name of the Lord as I give thanks to God through Him. Though the word "worship" is a noun, it does include an active state of being where I am continually presenting myself as a living sacrifice to God!

My life as a worshiper begins in my closet but leaks out and touches every area in which I allow Jesus to reign. Once I acknowledge the priority of abiding in Him in private, I must see past the futile attempts I've made to keep Him locked in the closet. Only then can I be an effective worshiper of the Living God in the mundane or the sensational of everyday public life.

The Father is seeking worshipers, so allow yourself to be sought! The personal fulfillment in this life is unbelievable and the rate of return is eternally valuable. Being conformed to the image of Jesus is the call of God upon each of His children. How He does that in each life is dependent on how we respond to the issues of His lordship. But know this...we are not professional Christians, as though it were our job to change ourselves. No, we simply spend time in His presence, obey what we've heard, and He does the work of producing the character of Christ in us. As He redeems the broken parts of us, we then are used for His redemptive purposes for others.

Meeting with the congregation of saints has many purposes for His Beloved. His plan for corporate worship is to bring us to new levels in our awareness of His eternal purposes, but we must have our personal relationship with Him in proper order to move forward into these purposes as a Body of believers. We must become true worshipers—those who withhold nothing from Him—to offer acceptable worship upon His altar.

Because Jesus has provided us an opportunity to fulfill all our personal longings for intimacy with Him in the secret place, I say get to know Him deeply and be changed by His radical love. The embrace of God is a priceless experience. Let's press on to *know Him* in private so we can *make Him known* in public.

Notes

1. Henri Nouwen, *The Way of the Heart* (New York, N.Y.: Ballentine Books, 1981), back cover.
2. Steve Fry, *A God Who Heals the Heart* (Brentwood, Tenn.: Deep Fryed Books, 1997), pp. 83-89.
3. Dutch Sheets, "Five Things to Keep Us Sharp," (Dallas, Tex.: November 19, 1997).
4. Andrew Murray, *Abide in Christ* (Springdale, Pa.: Whitaker House, 1979), n.p.

WORSHIP IS...?

All to Jesus I surrender, all to Him I freely give.
I will ever love and trust Him, in His presence daily live.
I surrender all. I surrender all.
All to Thee, my blessed Savior, I surrender all.

"I SURRENDER ALL"
BY JUDSON W. VAN DE VENTER AND WINFIELD S. WEEDON

Far too many Christians believe that worship is something that transpires between 10 A.M. and 12 noon on Sundays. However, worship, as we've already seen, is much more than giving two hours a week to the service of the sanctuary. The heathen can do that on Sundays at various shrines: restaurants, theaters, sports centers...you name it! But the children of the Almighty God have a much greater privilege. Knowing Him through daily worship is a redemptive provision of the new covenant where we can literally take on the characteristics of the God we worship...that is, we become partakers of His divine nature (see 2 Pet. 1:4).

Worship Is...Becoming Like Him

If God has predestined us to be conformed to the image of His Son, then He must have a plan for doing that. And throughout the centuries, key church leaders have offered us a variety of ways to accomplish this—everything from fasting and prayer to Scripture memory and feeding the poor. These acts, of course, are wonderful biblical examples of how to act like Jesus, but worship is much more.

You've seen the youth "groupies" of our day who magnify their favorite musical band. Before long, the posters on the wall, the clothes in the closet and the hairstyles start reflecting the, uh, "look" of that group or artist. What takes place here is the worship of an icon or an idol that begins to transform the individual into a clone of the one they worship. In the same way, as we truly worship the God of Glory, we are allowed to take on the characteristics of God's holiness that sets us apart from the worship of every other god. What an awesome way to become like Jesus!

Worship Is...Treasuring God

So what is worship? Worship is treasuring God. It is allowing ourselves to value Him, His words, His deeds and His thoughts far above those of others and ourselves. "Worthship" is the old English word that is still sometimes used today. It means placing worth on something. Perhaps you've heard it used as a title when addressing someone of high rank, "Your Worthship" or "Your Worship." Worship is seeing what God is worth and then giving Him due honor and adoration.

To say that we treasure God means that what He says and how He feels about things matters immensely to us. Nonetheless, we're not going to know what those things are unless we have cultivated the time necessary to listen to His opinions. When a person, place or thing is treasured, it is sought after as a valuable possession worthy of being obtained—even at a high price.

People magazine has featured several articles describing Sotheby's auctions where personal belongings of famous celebrities were sold at astronomical prices. It's incredible how much money some people will pay for the most eternally insignificant items. I once read that a woman spent her life savings (and that of her sister) to obtain specific pieces of Jackie Kennedy Onassis's costume jewelry. They weren't even real jewels!

I am reminded of times when friends and I played "pirates" as a kid. We would have good pirates and bad pirates...as if we could differentiate the two. The good ones were on a quest to find buried treasure with their secret map while the bad ones would try to thwart the progress of the good. When whatever we deemed to be the treasure was found, we would spend the rest of our time defending it. The fun was in pretending to give our lives for the sake of "the treasure." Its value became the objective of our make-believe world.

Then, thanks to Walt Disney, our make-believe world became a reality when he built the "Pirates of the Caribbean" attraction at Disneyland. Finally we could go to Los Angeles and get lost in a childhood dream with the re-creation of seventeenth-century anarchy, replete with pirates, ships, cannons and treasure chests. No wonder it has been the most popular attraction for years: You've got all the wonder of Peter Pan and Captain Hook combined with the adventure and nobility of finding something valuable—albeit selfishly looted and lavished.

As believers in an eternal realm, what is valuable to us? Jesus says, "And this is eternal life, that they may know Thee, the only true God, and Jesus Christ whom Thou hast sent" (John 17:3). Knowing God is eternal life. It's not some distant ethereal experience someplace after we die. It's NOW! Knowing God is NOW. Stepping into divine destiny with God is happening as you read, and the value of developing this life with God now is priceless. Preparation for forever is currently underway as the worship and adoration of God is something that will continue throughout eternity. We may as well get used to it here! It's valuable!

Worship Is...Giving to God

Psalm 96:7 says, "Ascribe to the Lord (give to the Lord) glory and strength." We "give" Him glory as we see Him to be the prominent recipient of who we are and what we have. We give Him strength by allowing HIS to become ours. Therefore, we don't boast in our accomplishments while in His presence. The giving of sacrifices in worship is the act of offering something of value to Him—particularly our lives. The truth is, God is worthy to receive all praise, glory, honor, power, wealth, wisdom and strength. And what about all the earthly things? Yes, He's also worthy to receive my time, money, weaknesses and my sin. He's worth everything I'm willing to give Him.

When I give Him my cares and my pain, that's also an effort of worship. It's one thing to give the Lord praise for something; it's entirely different to give Him my weaknesses and struggles. I'm saying, "Lord, You're big enough to take care of this situation in my life. I worship and esteem Your ability to see far beyond my present circumstances. I'm not able to carry the load of my life alone, so I give it to You." Suddenly, He becomes Lord again as I acknowledge Him as my helper and friend.

Worship Is...Dethroning Idols

Worship is transferring our affections from temporary false comforts (also known as idols) and placing them upon God. What are some of those temporary comforts we gravitate toward? To what or to whom do you turn after a bad day? Do you head for the refrigerator or the television to escape your pain? Are you satiated by food, sports, an "escape novel" or some other gratification mechanism? Please don't misunderstand the point. None of these things are evil in their appropriate context. Yet if I use them to anesthetize the frustration of my day and hide from God during my "chill out" times, they become addictions. When I acknowledge that my discomforts make me want to run away from reality into fantasy, however, I create an opportunity to "hide" in God and receive His comfort.

Thus, repentance is a form of worship. When I see the futility of the meaningless and worthless effects these false comforts have produced, I transfer my affections back to the true and living

God. He in turn shows me the truth of His life that supersedes that of the natural realm. I again come face-to-face with the meaning of true love which casts out fear. Seeing and acting on the truth becomes worship.

Affections are more than emotional dispositions that motivate me—they include desires, ambitions, lusts for things and my plans to obtain them. When I see God for who He is amid the occasional chaos of my life, my mind, will and emotions are affected. When I am in His presence and He makes Himself known, He touches me emotionally and affectionately. Yet, if I don't allow the Holy Spirit to affect my will and change my self-sufficient mind-set, I leave His presence virtually unchanged, having had only a brief moment of emotional indulgence with the Creator. He desires more than that. Jonathan Edwards once said in essence that if we don't find that our affections have moved from earthly idols toward God, we haven't truly worshiped.

True worship, again, is submitting all that I am to God. When I am so graciously met by the reality of God in the stillness of my private time of devotion, I see one more time that I need His gentle reminder throughout the day that I belong to Him. Such reassurance occurs in those times as He shows me I'm not doing "the Christian thing" by myself. It's a great comfort to know He's guiding me all along the way without any height-ened expectations of a skydive or a leap through the infamous fiery hoop.

Tim Keller, pastor of Redeemer Presbyterian Church in New York, offers the following view of worship:

Worship is grasping a truth about God and then letting it strike you in the center of your being. It thrills you—comforts you. That's when the truth has moved from left to right brain—from mind to heart. On the spot it will change the way you "feel." And from that moment on it will change the way you act. The whole brain, the whole person is affected.[1]

Most of us get hung up on God's expectations of us rather than His acceptance of us. We forget that He created us human beings, not human doings. Still our predisposition toward performance and production too often finds its way translated into our activities for God. It's difficult for us to just "be" without "doing" something that looks holy. We've applied the Scripture "faith without works is useless" (see Jas. 2:17,20) to every area of religious work. Sad enough, our works have now exceeded our faith and the very thing that was meant to motivate us now keeps us running an exhausting race. Who can keep up? What are we trying to prove? Have we misplaced the call to just "be"?

There's nothing wrong with doing good things for God. We must stay motivated as we provoke one another to love and good works (see Heb. 10:24). However, incessant religious activity can easily become another idol that tries to replace genuine love for God.

It's easy for us to get caught up in the activity of worship. It even becomes a safe place at times when we can't handle the pressure of His presence which requires more of us than we think we're able to give. Subconsciously we think, *If I can just keep up this activity, I won't have to deal with the feelings of inadequacy and fear that aloneness with God produces. I'd rather remain on the outside and be safe than to be inside and frightened!* Choices! Once we realize what we're doing, is there really a choice to be made? Can we afford to remain distant from Him and totally miserable?

Are you struggling with substituting activity for relationship? If so, please join me in the following prayer:

Dear Lord Jesus,
Please deliver me from the trap where mere activities try to prove me a worshiper. I acknowledge that I've fallen prey to an idol-building mentality with "holy activity" at the top of the worship list. I've become enamored with the things I can do for You which replace my "first love" conviction of just being with You. I'm coming to an under-

standing that there is no performance available that can counteract or correct a faulty belief system in You as a loving Father. I don't want to hide from you any longer. I choose, once again, to see You as You truly are: arms outstretched waiting for my response to Your embrace to rest in You. Thank You for healing me! In Jesus' name. Amen.

Worship Is...Faith Focused

Our humanity often dictates that we see life through "soulish"-colored glasses. That's the nature of the carnal man. Not necessarily evil, just carnal. The things we perceive by way of our five senses become the pseudo-spiritual standard of judgment. If it doesn't make sense to our natural minds, we then must enter the realm of faith—or believing in something we cannot see, feel or understand. That's where God lives! And He will see to it that we are led into that realm before He shows us very much of His character. We wouldn't have the capacity to grasp it otherwise.

Constant pain in our lives related to unresolved issues with God and others is antagonistic toward the holiness and wholeness of God. These issues aim to keep us out of God's healing presence and waste our time in the wilderness.

For those of us who have been a bit apprehensive of that realm of faith, we find it intensely intimidating to "blindly trust" a God who has guaranteed nothing but His presence in the process. Therefore we "reserve the right" to trust Him or not trust Him, depending on the circumstance. We then begin to maneuver on an apparatus of arrogance as we read the Bible and decide whether or not we want to comply. Besides the overall and general conclusion that we are faith deficient due to our sinful human nature, specifically what is it that keeps us from fully trusting Him? What keeps us from the One who alone can transform the hideous into holy?

Many of us have carried around deep wounds and scars from the past that have hindered our liberty in responding to the Lord in worship. The nice word to call these things is "distractions" in the Holy Place. But let's face it—constant pain in our lives related to unresolved issues with God and others is antagonistic toward the holiness and wholeness of God. These issues aim to keep us out of God's healing presence and waste our time in the wilderness. The problem is that most us don't realize what the issues are. Nevertheless, they are anti-Christ in purpose to withhold the life of Jesus from us. Demonically inspired or not, they are evil and must be viewed as such.

Dealing with those things can take time, energy and commitment to the fire of God's presence and truth before a genuine breakthrough comes. Challenging though it may be, if we are committed to seeing wholeness in our lives, God will see to it that "the sun of Righteousness rises with healing in His wings" (Mal. 4:2) to carry us to that place of promise. He wants us to be free and fully able to come to Him with every concern. And He's ready to move heaven and earth to accomplish that for YOU and me. What a promise!!

Hindrances to Worship

Because we have this great promise, I decided to take a brief survey, asking people what they felt were the greatest hindrances to personal worship. A large percentage said, "intimidation" and "self-consciousness." Still, just as serious were the responses of "fear" and "shame." Hearing responses from other men was no new revelation to me, based on the knowledge of myself as a regular kind of guy. Yet I knew of several other areas of bondage based on my own experiences that contributed to the lack of personal devotion in the average "Joe Christian." Let's explore a few of them together.

Unbelief

As I began to break this down into smaller morsels, I realized that one of the greatest problems in worship is pride—and pride finds its roots in the sin of unbelief. Especially for us men, who struggle with a self-expectation to "do it" all right, whatever IT is. The analytical mind sees personal worship as a task that must be calculated before it can be undertaken and mastered, rationalizing:

This is a job and must be taken seriously with periodic progress reports. The performance aspect is important to me and I need to know that the monitoring process is fair. That's why prayer journals are one way to prove to myself that I'm a disciplined specimen, worthy to receive favor from God. This devotion thing is aimed at what I can do for God. So I must do it well to achieve the desired effect.

What I'm really saying, however, is that I don't believe God is truly interested in me and my needs. In my heart I know I desperately need the loving arms of Jesus to enfold me and let me know that I don't have to do it all right. God knows the expectations from family and coworkers are enough to daily drain me.

So the unbelief factor becomes just as paralyzing as any other evil influence. Does Jesus really want to touch me or just change me so I can be a better person for Him? What more can I give to this God who has everything anyway? There must be more, but what else must I do to please Him? Work...work... work...UGH!

Feelings of Inadequacy

Improper views of ourselves fit into this category of pride. Behind the inflated facade of confident airs is usually an escape mechanism. I find it hard to ignore the painful reality that I'm not yet who I want to be. A biblical example of this is found in the book of Romans. On the heels of instructing the Church to present their bodies as living sacrifices, Paul says, "And do not be conformed to this world, but be transformed by the renewing of your mind, that you may prove what the will of God is, that which is good and acceptable and perfect....I say to every man among you not to think more highly of himself than he ought to think" (Rom. 12:2,3).

It's true that many of us see ourselves differently than God sees us. Some of us view ourselves more highly than we ought, but just as many saints (if not more) fight paralyzing feelings of worthlessness and inadequacy in the presence of God. This extreme humility is really an inverted pride that finds difficulty receiving help from God. All of life is seen as a direct result of that person's actions or attitudes. "It's all my fault" is their motto. Regularly listening to the voice of the accuser, these people tend to believe the worst about themselves in most situations and will seek every method possible to prove that they are accurate in their perception of how horrible they really are. Jesus' words, "Blessed are the poor in spirit, for theirs is the kingdom of heaven" (Matt. 5:3) becomes perverted (turned inside out) as they strive toward the humiliation of self-flagellation.

These individuals perceive God's grace as available to them only when they've exhausted every other possible fleshly effort and resource. Trying to worship from this position welcomes strange fire upon the altar (see Num. 16) and completely short-circuits the enabling power of the Spirit. Wheel-spinning trophies are then distributed to those who perspire the most! Shame ultimately becomes the master and the motivating force behind this drive to succeed in flying-leap attempts toward holiness. One day when the light switch is turned on, it will become very clear that they worshiped the "standard" and not God at all.

We must see that the power of God's presence can utterly shatter that image and destroy it like the idol of Dagon in his temple when the Ark of the Covenant was present (see 1 Sam.

5:4). If, through repentance, we allow the Holy Spirit to purge and cleanse us from all false gods, this too can fall. No more worshiping at the altar of self-denial. Denial of self is a means to an end...to be closer to Jesus, not to earn brownie points for a fasted life!

Fear of Being Known

True, intimidation and self-consciousness are destructive in the pursuit of God but fear plays an equally destructive role. Graham Kendrick writes a fitting story that applies to this issue of fear:

> It was the little boy's first trip to church, and his mother had hurriedly put him through the correct "Sunday best" procedure of thorough washing, dressing in smart clothes, and the inventing of a parting in his hair—previously unknown to his startled scalp. Having been warned to "behave," which generally meant "shut up and don't fidget," they proceeded to the local church under the incessant clanging of its bell.
>
> On entering the church, the boy was instantly curious, fascinated by this strange new world. The hushed voices, the high arches, the slightly musty smell and the rows of empty wooden pews. Or were they empty? No, here and there a hat, the back of a head, a pair of hunched shoulders, would bob up or down, appear or disappear.
>
> His mother led him in whispers to one of these dark tunnel-like rows, where she immediately knelt and bowed her head; he copied instinctively. The silence only lasted for a few more seconds, as the question that had been growing more and more urgent in his lively young mind suddenly burst out, ringing loud and clear through the ancient arches: "Mummy, who are we all hiding from?"[2]

Indeed! Who were these people hiding from? Is this indicative of the camouflaged inner fear so many live with in their approach to God the Father? If asked, would we realize it or be honest enough to say, "Yes, I'm afraid of God!"? (Perhaps I shall be the first.)

I grew up afraid of God for a number of reasons, most beyond my control. I knew that I loved God (or thought I did), and I never wanted to do anything to make Him angry with me. I was a good boy...just ask my mom! Despite the good things I was taught at home and in Sunday School about the mercy and love of God, many of them didn't translate well into my young heart and mind.

I believed I could keep God happy by doing good things for Him. When I would hear sermons about the anger and wrath of God against sin, I took them personally and knew that He had to be mad at me for something. This was an improper fear of the Lord. Of course I never said anything about this to my parents because I was too ashamed of myself for being imperfect. I didn't know it was okay to be human. My only recourse was to continue my spotless performance for God in hopes that He would overlook the negative things in me and respect my "fear" of Him.

I was able to continue this charade until my energy left and life as I knew it ceased. I had to stop and discover the true and living God I had never known. No more hiding out of fear! God saw to it that I faced Him completely naked. In His pure love for me, He sought me out and found me, wretched as I was, alone and frightened. Then He began to reveal an enormous fear I had...ME! I was afraid of God AND me. I was so ashamed of what I saw in myself that it frightened me to think I may never be able to change. Little did I know at the time that God would use that very fear of myself to reveal His overcoming power in me.

Fear of Father God

Wrong concepts of Father God fit into this category of fear. There are several kinds of fear found in the Scriptures and for those who have struggled with the idea of the fear of God, I would recommend a thorough study of the character of the Father from the Word of God. Because we derive our identity and sense of worth and well-being from our fathers, those who've had unhealthy father figures in their lives will tend to superimpose that image onto God the Father. This is a serious stumbling block to healthy worship. You can never truly worship God through natural understanding alone. Eventually that method will backfire and God will come storming out of His box to make a simple point....He cannot be contained in temples made with hands nor can He be reduced to man's well-constructed philosophies.

Some have viewed Him as an ethereal being who lives in another galaxy and shows up on the planet once every few hundred years. Others see Him as the mean daddy who looks over their shoulder and just waits for them to blow it. Still others see Him as a businessman or employer who expects them to punch a clock and do their job...well!

The worship of God based on nothing but a phobia of Him produces an anemic if not a fatalistic relationship. This phobia at its core is an accusation against God and His ways. The phobia of God shouts, "I can't trust You to know what is best for my life. Therefore, I must take care of myself!" Self-sufficiency becomes the quintessential avenue of existence, and paying lip-service to an Almighty God on Sunday morning is a necessity to prove that following the rules looks good on one's spiritual resumé. Self-consciousness is directly related to the fear of man and goes hand in hand with "God phobia." And "the fear of man brings a snare" (Prov. 29:25). Joy Dawson says it this way:

> The fear of man is being more impressed with man's reaction to our actions than with God's reaction. That's bondage. When we have the fear of God upon us, we are impressed only with God's reaction. We are freed from the concern of what people think. That's freedom! That's release! That's great relief![3]

A healthy fear and respect of the Lord is to hate evil. To hate evil is to hate the things that draw my attention away from pursuing a holy passion for God. What desires do I have that try to replace the satisfaction God desires for me to find in Him? What occupies the passionate place in my heart that displaces Jesus?

Passion for Jesus is cultivated and nurtured as I create time to shut myself away with Him. When God reveals Himself and shows what proper respect and fear of Him is, my life is completely transformed and true worship takes on a whole new complexion. God-consciousness becomes the true fear of the Lord. And "the fear of the Lord is the beginning of wisdom" (Ps. 111:10).

Fear of Intimacy

As we've already discussed, men usually find it more difficult to lower their masculine barriers when expressing their true feelings about something. But don't be fooled. Many women have the same if not greater difficulties in sharing their deep feelings. Though they can be labeled "pride" or "fear of intimacy" issues, the truth is something deep in the wounded spirit that has produced either a damaged identity or a loss of identity. Being comfortable with the real you becomes terribly difficult because you may never have been allowed to be you.

The Lord is opposed to anything that keeps us apart from Him. He desires to...heal the memory that has kept us from being who He created us to be.

As emotional creatures, we were created to express feelings. When this natural response is repressed, for whatever reason, it's not easy to recover the instinct and operate in it freely again without a touch from God.

The expectations of others, whether family or friends, have produced a false sense of self. The only "safe" way to live has been to conceal who you are—if you know who that is—and not share the deep parts of you for fear of the rejection. Whatever the situation, the Lord is opposed to anything that keeps us apart from Him. He desires to delve deep into the realm of that painful experience and heal the memory that has kept us from being *who* He created us to be.

Although the pain of the past can keep us from being honest with ourselves, the Lord is committed to showing His love in the midst of life's detours. Freedom from its perils comes in accepting the person God created, complete with all our faults and fears. No more hiding! Honesty with God in private communion, even little pieces at a time, breaks down the false intimacy we have developed with ourselves. We think we have a good relationship with ourselves until we find it difficult to be honest with God who knows us best. Knowing Him and becoming comfortable with yourself can be a simultaneously fulfilling experience when you allow yourself the luxury of a regular date with God.

Sin Patterns

Here's another obvious, but often overlooked, hindrance to worship. Many people who wrestle with life-dominating sin patterns—stumbling frequently and defeated in every sense of the word—rarely come into a worship experience. When they do take that bold step of faith, it's usually to do a good deed in order to seek freedom from depression and oppression.

God's presence is readily available to set us free from such things. However, depression and oppression are often related to, or are a consequence of, sin. We must also realize that in many cases, depression is a result of anger and fear. Sin by its nature causes depression. When we sin, we have anger toward ourselves for falling into sin's trap, accompanied by the fear of its consequences. Thus, we become mortified over the guilt of sin and allow its power to keep us from God—the only One who can deliver us from its strangulating hold. Shame then gains a foothold that says, "Not only did you do something awful, you're an awful person. Jesus could never really love you enough to provide a way out of this mess—but if He did, you're not strong enough to walk out. You're deceived to think that you'll ever really be free from this habit. God does not want to be with you when you're like this."

The old broken record of lies is reinforced because we've listened to it so repetitiously! And boy do we believe it. The very things we need are elusive because of our shame. We allow ourselves to be driven from God's presence like Adam and Eve from the garden when we should instead be running *toward* Him. The enemy uses every vile tactic in his demonic arsenal to keep us in a cycle of fear and doubt to circumvent our discovering the wholeness offered in God's presence.

We need only cry out to God in those times, to hear the blood of Jesus speak louder than the blood of bulls and goats and allow the Holy Spirit to lead us to the Cross. Repentance can be simply responding to the Spirit's enlightenment of the Word in our lives. Our response determines our success as overcomers. Times of true repentance and emotionally healing prayer with a spiritual leader or a faithful trusted friend are essential to breaking free. Joy Dawson says it this way:

> The level of our repentance of sin will depend upon the degree to which we see sin as God sees it and hate it as God hates it....Repentance means a change of mind, a change of heart, and a change of life toward sin.[4]

If we can see sin as something that keeps us from obtaining God's best for our lives, we can learn to hate it as He does. God warmly welcomes us to come boldly into His presence if we accept His prescribed method through the cleansing blood of Jesus. The preparation we make to enter into His gates with thanksgiving and His courts with praise is in regularly identifying with the sacrifice of Jesus. To say that I've "accepted the

Lord" is to say that I accept His sacrifice for the penalty of my sin. I accept that I cannot do anything to earn the grace of God except trust in Jesus' blood. My life is in His hands for I belong to Him!

My confession is: "I have been crucified with Christ; and it is no longer I who live, but Christ lives in me; and the life which I now live in the flesh I live by faith in the Son of God, who loved me, and delivered Himself up for me" (Gal. 2:20). This opens the door for me to give myself to God as an offering of worship.

Worship Is...Abiding in the Vine

Whether it be within the confines of my date with God or in the congregation of the saints, the lips that offer the sweet fruit of thanks to His name must speak the same language as the tree of Life Himself. If He says, "Come unto Me," I must say, "To You I will come." I must choose the life He offers if I am to grow as a fruit-producing branch from the Vine. Abiding in the Vine produces the fruit of that Vine without a struggle. Just as apple trees naturally produce apples, staying connected to Jesus naturally and supernaturally produces the fruit of worship in my life.

I was created for this! To offer myself as worship to God. Daily. Although it is possible to worship Him and not really know Him, it is nearly impossible to know Him and not truly worship Him. Like the chicken and the egg, what comes first— knowing Him or worshiping Him? Whatever the answer to that question is, time spent in private worship and devotion can only improve my knowledge of God and my desire to worship Him. If indeed He has the words of life, where else could I go to find the freedom to live?

Notes

1. Tim Keller, "What It Takes to Worship Well" (*Leadership*, Spring 1994), pp. 17-23.
2. Graham Kendrick, *Learning to Worship As a Way of Life* (Minneapolis, Minn.: Bethany House Publishers, 1984), pp. 11-15.
3. Joy Dawson, *Intimate Friendship with God* (Old Tappan, N.J.: Chosen Books, 1986), p. 33.
4. Ibid, p. 57.

CELEBRATING WITH THE CONGREGATION

We are God's people, the chosen of the Lord.
Born of His Spirit, established by His Word;
Our Cornerstone is Christ alone, and strong in Him we stand;
Oh let us live transparently, and walk heart to heart
and hand in hand.

"WE ARE GOD'S PEOPLE"
BY BRYAN JEFFERY LEECH AND JOHANNES BRAHMS

By now I hope you're strongly convinced that a foundation of personal devotion and private worship is crucial to the flow of Jesus' life in us. This "love affair" with the Son of God is literally the lifeline that connects us to our eternal destiny around the throne. The mutual love exchanged between the Bride and the Bridegroom is the "missing link" to the cosmic fulfillment of the ages. Almost sounds like a futuristic romance novel! Well, why not?

This divine romance between God and humanity has been challenged on every side by the rulers of this world since the beginning of time. The age-old battle between light and darkness has been waged to keep the love of God concealed. But today we're seeing a widespread revival of pure love and passion for the Son of God that could quite possibly supersede that of all previous generations.

Keeping the Romance Alive

When you love someone, your daily thoughts are captivated by that person. You meditate on innovative ways to express your love in word and deed. Time stops in the presence of real love, and time deepens its roots. Between husband and wife, the true test of love comes after you've been married for a number of years. If romance is not guarded as a treasure, couples tend to take one another for granted and gradually lose the spark of love that once characterized their marriage. Many have learned this lesson the hard way and have lost a valuable treasure by taking advantage of the gift of love in a mate. The Lord used the grave mistake I made in my own marriage to show me the lack of value I also placed on my relationship with Him.

Today as an "educated" romantic, I go through seasons of creative intimacy with my wife, Laurie. Sometimes I like to show up at home with some flowers or a small gift just to let her know that I'm thinking about her. It's even fun to mail a card to her. In the middle of the day when she gets the mail, there's a note from me that says she is special and means the world to me. That's so much more romantic to her than an occasional phone call. I really don't need a specific reason to send flowers or a card. I simply love her! She's precious to me every day—not just on special occasions.

Likewise, the Lord is good every day and I don't need a special reason to tell Him how I feel. Besides the obvious reasons of saving me from death and giving me a purpose for living, I think the Lord likes it when for no apparent reason I just burst into telling Him how great He is...how wonderful His presence is...or how sweet His love is to me. This is spontaneity at its height as I "Romance the (Corner) Stone"!

Factoring in the Family

If the marriage relationship is a picture of the relationship between Jesus and the Church (as most Christian wedding ceremonies state), then there is an inference of romance built into that picture. However, as the love relationship grows into a season of procreation, other responsibilities arise. Children produce a whole new set of duties and blessings. But even in the midst of family joy, longings to be alone with the love of your life still exist.

For example, once in a while I like to plan times when Laurie and I can just "get away." We are refreshed by times of intimacy without having to think about all the other chores of adulthood and parenthood. It invigorates me to just "chill out" with my wife. Still, there are those times when I know we must take care of family business. It's not just "me and my honey" then. It's me, Honey and the four bambinos. God has placed a responsibility on me to develop us into a family. I am to provide a healthy environment where everyone is given the opportunity to learn and grow in their responses to the tasks of daily life. Those times can be mutually fulfilling for us as we encourage one another—the older helping the younger.

To keep everyone safe and protected, we have a few rules in our house. They are simply, "Honor God, honor people and honor people's things." All the commandments of God can fit into one or another of these categories. Adherence to these simple rules keeps things flowing smoothly between us as a family. From time to time the Lord shows us things that need to change or improve, and to the best of our ability, we follow His leading.

The Framework of Family

Within the framework of our family dynamics, I've noticed the intimacy factor between Laurie and me is different when we're dealing with the children. We do not expect one another to meet the depths of our emotional needs while we are conducting family business. My first priority is for the well-being of the family as a whole before I look for my personal, individual needs to be met. When I come home from the office my first concern is how things are on the homefront. Is everyone and everything OK? I care about how my wife and children handled the day. What action should we take, if any, with the problems that have arisen? What praise is necessary or what correction must be administered?

As a father, I relate to my children as a nurturer, a problem solver and a disciplinarian. Those roles are important to our family structure, and the growth of their internal value systems to keep them safe and secure. Because the children are still relatively young, I cannot compromise the well-being of the family unit simply because I don't "feel like" assuming my responsibilities. When we have matters to discuss that involve everyone, we ask for and respect everyone's opinion. When one has a personal need, I try to handle it on an individual basis.

After we've settled into the evening I find my desires for rest and intimate conversation with my wife falling into place and proper order. We've taken care of family business with the children who are now busy with homework or chores, and we can now relate on a different level. The day began with, "Good morning, Honey," and it ends with, "Phew! We made it through another day. How are you, my love?"

A Time for God, a Time for His Family

Likewise, my intimate life with God has a proper place, even though throughout the years I've found myself displacing and projecting my need for God onto others. What the Lord wanted to do in me privately, He couldn't do because I wasn't giving Him the opportunity. My expectation was that godly people could meet those needs in the congregational (family) setting. This was completely reasonable to me, as I was a "people person." I naturally assumed God would use His people to satisfy the deep need for Himself that exists in every heart. I managed to conceal that large, gaping wound in my heart with an expectation that others would be able to fill and heal the "need-for-God" deficit in me. It was a painfully rude awakening to find out that Jesus alone was the answer!

Family Focus Begins with the Father

But putting Father first does not come without a struggle. Through the natural process of human development, pediatric psychology tells us that one of the first things children are aware of is self. The needs of the body are paramount: food, rest, shelter and affirmation. Though the carnal man is most aware of himself, the spirit of man is most aware of God—the Creator of self. As we grow in the Lord, we become more aware of our role as needy children. And through the maturing process, we see that we cannot remain in that totally helpless state. We must grow up into the full stature of Christ (see Eph. 4:13)...as a mature man or woman. It is only when we mature that we can take our eyes off of self and focus on the Father and His family.

Sandra (not her real name) was visiting our services for the first time and was quite exuberant about it. She had heard about the powerful worship and teaching of the Word at our church, and was anxious to visit our congregation. After a few visits, however, she approached me with some genuine concerns about our fellowship. I quickly realized that what she needed from our times in worship was not what she got. I felt some unhealthy demands being placed on me as the worship leader, and knowing nothing about her created a slight internal caution that made me listen a lot before speaking.

Sadly, I later discovered that Sandra was a single woman with a grim history of abuse which translated into serious "father" issues that were impossible for others to fix in a given service of worship. The need in her life constituted a progressive revelation of God's love and acceptance of her just as she was, and a truth of the Scriptures that would give her a broader perspective of worship's purpose. My heart was broken for her as I saw the debilitating truth that she really wanted people to do what only God could do. And what God would be allowed to do would take some time...but only if she were willing.

I soon got the impression Sandra was expecting the corporate worship time to meet the emotional needs that only her private time with the Father could meet. I attempted to reach her with practical reason but quickly realized that she needed more than an explanation. No need to wax theologically eloquent in any discourse of rhetoric....Sandra needed a solid relationship with the Lord to bring her out of the bondage of relying on others to pronounce her "worthy." God had her number and was getting ready to heal the father wound in her.

Challenging Sandra to allow the Lord access to her private world was initially met with some resistance but she said she would prayerfully consider it. What more could I ask for?! Her growth began slowly, but after a few weeks I saw something promising. As the healing power of Jesus was released to her in private, Sandra's need for personal intimacy with God in public was not as pronounced. Soon she began to embrace the purpose of approaching God together instead of alone in our corporate worship services. In time she even started seeing that God had more in store for congregational worship than just individual fulfillment.

Father's Perspective on Family Gatherings

Technically, corporate worship (family gatherings) is for God's purposes rather than for our own. Therefore we need not get upset if our personal lists for emotional gratification are not satisfied in the service. If our "worship buttons" are not pressed properly, do we find our enjoyment level rapidly declining? We must determine what our main objective is in joining the congregation for worship, then possibly change our perspectives to fit our beliefs. God desires first to work in us in private before working through us in public. We cannot depend on a once a week "dose of life" in corporate worship to accomplish all He wants to do in us through private worship. There's so much more grace available throughout the other six days of the week.

When we gather for our weekly worship times, we congregate for more than just a spiritual fix. God has entrusted His people with some serious privileges and responsibilities. As His family, we find joy gathering in His presence, but our family times are more than a careless, lighthearted event—they are times to deal with family issues. We must be aware that there are:

- sins to confess;
- mercies to entreat;
- battles to be waged;
- praises to be sung;
- areas of lordship to be acknowledged; and
- encouragement and correction to be administered.

Our primary function as God's covenant people in a given location is to recognize His worth and minister to Him. To wait upon Him, listening for what He desires and asking what would please Him most at that particular time: "How can I best serve you, my Master? How can I best acknowledge Your desires and fulfill them?" This is the kind of individual He looks for in a worship service.

Misconceptions About Family (Corporate) Worship

Sunday's worship time is when we gather to share the things that have become fundamental to our lives throughout the week. And it's important that we celebrate together! Hebrews 10:23-25 makes it clear that God is not just suggesting we gather with those of His household to worship together. The writer begins with an encouragement to hold on to the confession of hope...to stimulate one another to love and good deeds and "not forsaking our own assembling together, as is the habit of some, but encouraging one another; and all the more, as you

> *In true worship God is preeminent and the center of our attention. Conversely, in false worship I am preeminent and my needs are the center of attention.*

see the day drawing near." This exhortation sounds like preparation for coming conflict or perhaps battle. It's spiritual boot camp for God's Kingdom Survival School.

It's About the Father, Not My Feelings

Yet many of us have viewed "church" as a time to receive warm feelings from God after a difficult week of fighting the devil...or the boss. Though the warm feelings are available, we often neglect the fact that ministry to the Lord takes us back to the first commandment which is to love the Lord our God with all our heart, mind, soul and strength (see Matt. 22:37). Naturally, being the first commandment, the Lord has placed holy significance on this one to consistently direct our focus back to Him. In true worship God is preeminent and the center of our attention. Conversely, in false worship I am preeminent and my needs are the center of attention.

You've probably guessed by now that corporate worship is NOT just an emotional feeling that makes you want to sing...nor should it be confused with nostalgia. Some base their worship experience on the comforts of warm memories that accompany a certain style of music or a favorite song. Many are moved to tears at the sound of "My Jesus, I Love Thee." Then again, others are similarly affected by the theme from Disney's "Beauty and the Beast." Are these worship responses? Probably not. They're most likely the effects of an emotional attachment to a pleasant experience. Worship should be a pleasant experience, and one that goes far beyond the limitations of a mentally and emotionally stimulating array of memory-making material.

It's About Change, Not Easing Our Consciences

Another misguided subconscious idea about corporate worship is that it is for the purpose of "conscience cleansing." The fact that some people go to church, sing the songs, confess their sins and put $20 in the offering, go home and feel better is NOT worship. Their consciences may be cleared by doing "the right thing" on Sunday but the presence of the Almighty has not been allowed to touch them to the brink of significant life changes. Unfortunately, many individuals repeat this behavior week after week and never truly worship God.

He Inhabits the Praises of His People

So what's the point of worshiping together? Does God *need* our worship? Does God *need* anything? According to Scripture we know that His eyes roam throughout the earth seeking those whose hearts are completely His. Still it's a bit ludicrous to even think that God has *need* of a thing. Yet God has ordained from the beginning that He be praised. Whether it be the angels in heaven, creation itself (including the rocks) or humankind, His name will be glorified:

> "For from the rising of the sun, even to its setting, My name will be great among the nations, and in every place incense is going to be offered to My name, and a grain offering that is pure; for My name will be great among the nations," says the Lord of hosts (Mal. 1:11).

As with various natural laws, God has ordained the laws of sowing and reaping and of gravity. He no longer needs to be actively involved in these laws because He's already set them in motion and upholds them simply by the power of the words He spoke ages ago.

A spiritual law already in motion is that of the praise to His name. He will be praised in the heavens and in the earth by something or someone—there is virtually no way around it. Now, of course, His greatest "desire" is to be worshiped by His greatest creation—humankind. Nevertheless, He gives us the choice.

When we choose to honor Him by giving Him the glory due His name, something powerful transpires. He turns His attention toward us and we are changed by an encounter with Him.

Bob Sorge, author of *Exploring Worship*, beautifully outlines the aspects of worship's purpose by setting up three general spheres:

- The vertical aspect of worship;
- The horizontal aspect;
- The inward aspect.

In this vertical aspect of worship...The very first and primary reason for worship is to minister to the Lord. The basic posture of the worshiper is, "I will bless You, Lord," not, "Lord, bless me!"...A second reason for our worship services is to realize the manifest presence of God in our midst...to provide an opportunity for the power of God to be released in His church....We also worship in order to provide an atmosphere or seedbed for the gifts of the Spirit and various spiritual ministries to be manifested....Finally we worship in order to open up the channels of communication between us and God.[1]

The fact that we worship makes a statement of what we believe about ourselves: We have need of a greater force than ourselves to carry us through this life. We are sinners and have need of a Savior.

The way in which we worship makes a statement about what we believe about our God: He's holy, worthy, awesome, mighty, loving and caring. The styles of music or the means by which we communicate the content of worship creates a sense of personality that is compatible with those of like heart and mind. Likewise, the strength of what we actually believe about God is energized by our ability to demonstrate, celebrate and proclaim the praise of Him who called us out of darkness into His marvelous light (see 1 Pet. 2:9).

Because we were created to worship God, the reasonable thought is that it's normal for us to express worship to Him. Unfortunately, through sin and the painful experiences of our lives, our worship instinct has gone awry, causing us to worship the wrong things: power, control, pleasure, comfort, self and "drugs of choice." Though most of us are not cognizant of worshiping Old Testament pagan gods such as Baal, Ashterah or Molech, the demonic spirits behind those ancient deities are still prevalent today and continue to war against the Church of the Living God.

The good news is, at the heart of an honest worship encounter with the Living God, whether it can be articulated or not, there is a rudimentary desire to be transformed by His incredible power. And He's ready to meet the hungry hearts of those who honestly present themselves to Him and are willing to receive His transforming love and power.

As a worshiper who has been sought after by God, I want to search for ways in which I can give myself and express my heart toward Him. I want to see Him as the object of my worship, the focus of my being and the purpose for life in general. The more freedom I receive to express these truths, the more I become transformed into the image God created for me—a free person. I literally become free to be me!

An active part of my love for God is in how I express my worship to Him. Psalm 149 begins and ends with, "Praise the

Lord!" What an incredible honor and privilege it is to praise the Lord of all creation, the Savior of our souls and the King of Life!

Expressing Praise

But what does it mean to praise the Lord? The Bible includes many different words for "praise." Many of us are familiar with some of the Hebrew words for praise that have changed the atmosphere of congregational worship throughout the past 25 years. Can you imagine what our corporate worship times would be like if we became comfortable with biblical worship expressions in our prayer closets first? Just think of the unity and freedom this would bring to our family gatherings!

Are you saying that I can do these things in my private time alone with God? YES! Who's the worship for anyway? Certainly not to prove how well you do it in public! Because I am a worshiper, not just one who offers worship, the audience is ONE and I must continue to ask myself the question, *Can I be satisfied with that?*

Whether it is in the privacy of home or in the corporate worship setting, the simple point is becoming comfortable with who I am in front of God in worship. Am I free to be who I am with Him, or must I "control" myself or even "muster up" some feelings in His presence? Can I tell Him how I really feel or should I reserve the truth for someone who won't judge me? Will I be graded on how holy I look or act when I'm with Him? (Fortunately, heaven's grading system will prove to be very different from ours! Remember, Father is looking for worshipers—not just worship!)

Singing

Singing is probably the most common vehicle of thanksgiving and testimony...and definitely the most acceptable. The Hebrew word *tehilim*, which is the title for the book of Psalms, comes from the word *tehillah* and actually means a hymn or song of praise. Though we've looked at this method of praise in an earlier chapter, praising God in song is a perfect way to strip off the effects of depression. Isaiah 61:3 promises that the garment of praise we receive from the Lord replaces the spirit of heaviness. If you haven't already, you ought to try it sometime! Next time you have a bad day (though you won't feel like doing this), sing praise to God for a while until the gloom lifts! It works! Once your attention is shifted from the temporal realm to the eternal, your soul will start to stabilize. You'll find that your mind gets clearer and you can think better.

Shouting

Shouting is a powerful way to express yourself in praise (but I would think twice before acting on this one at 6 A.M. in an apartment!). The two main words in Hebrew are *rua´* and *shava´*—both meaning to shout, to cry out, to address in a loud tone or to commend. Culturally, this method of praise is relatively unacceptable in America except at sports or social events. (I've not tried this one when commending my wife or children.)

Think about it for a moment, though. On Saturday we rave at the ball field for our favorite athletic team, and yet on Sunday we become stifled and quiet in church. Do you see a problem with this picture? Shouting unto God in praise of His glorious victories is just as reverent as singing a quiet hymn about His love. No difference! Can you identify with the sense of release that is experienced over the deafening screams and cheers as the favored team scores? Something happens to us when we release the shout to God.

Clapping

The effect is similar when we clap our hands. When we applaud an action we're saying that we approve of the participants' performance and we are proud to be part of the experience. Though used only once in Scripture as a directive for praise, the power of this expression is utilized in every realm of our social and recreational lives—and in virtually every culture. To applaud the Lord is to make a joyful noise to Him. We recognize His accomplishments and we say they are good. Well done, God! We are proud of You!

Ministry to the Lord in corporate worship provides opportunity for the Spirit to impart holy life to us and to birth God-breathed vision and strategies into a people who will be obedient to carry out His plans.

Lifting Our Hands

One of the most intimate words for praise used in the Old Testament is *yadah,* meaning to revere by stretching out one's hands. This word is possibly related to the word *yada',* which means "to know" someone and can be used to describe the intimacy in the private chambers of a husband and wife. *Yada'* is used when Adam "knew" Eve and she conceived. This aspect of intimacy with the Father in worship has a seriously warm and loving overtone. I see His heart for His creation coming through. His invitation for us to know Him in worship has to be the most intimate appeal from heaven's throne. When I lift my hands to Him, I am accepting His embrace of me just as I am. Can it get any warmer or more intimate than that?

Corporate Intimacy Results in the Birth of the Corporate Vision

Corporate intimacy occurs when the congregation as a whole comes into an awareness of God's embrace. In those times it seems that His love is as physically tangible as liquid love. Enjoying these blissful moments we think, *What an awesome experience.* How can we possibly go home and forget about it? What is happening in those very moments is a holy corporate conception. The infusing of this kind of life into a congregation is very unique and miraculous. When the Holy Spirit hovers over a group of people, it's the same as He did over Mary to conceive in her the promise.

Have you ever wondered why the vision tarries or why it seems to be taking so long for the Lord to keep His promises to us as a local fellowship? What's wrong? We've prayed and believed for months and even years. Still, no fruit. Consider this: If there is no corporate intimacy with God, there can be no conception—thus, no birthing of the vision.

Ministry to the Lord in corporate worship provides opportunity for the Spirit to impart holy life to us and to birth God-breathed vision and strategies into a people who will be obedient to carry out His plans. Remember though, the Holy Spirit cannot plant seeds of life into an immature womb. If the Bride of Christ is not prepared, she cannot conceive! God's people must be prepared personally to receive corporately. This is the daily availability we talked about earlier that gives us "license" to expect God's visitations.

Humility Comes Before Honor

God visits those who come to Him in a spirit of humility. Humility invokes God's favor. Scripture says that God resists the proud but gives grace to the humble (see Jas. 4:6). Much to our disappointment, humility is not an innate human characteristic. We are prone to prove our worth, slap the opposition and make a name for ourselves. It's important for us to be in the top 10! And as the recent Olympics shows, the top 3 is preferable. To give place to another over ourselves requires great humility, and to allow someone else the place in line ahead of us is almost unheard of.

Humility is seeing ourselves clearly. I've heard it said,

"Humility is the vigorous state of knowing who you are...and more importantly, who you are NOT." Knowing who we are and who we are not in God's presence is essential for growth in our knowledge of Him.

Humbling ourselves before God is not just seeing but responding with our hearts and bodies—this includes posture. The Hebrew word *barak* means both to kneel and to bless God as an act of adoration. And yet, we seldom see time set aside for kneeling or bowing in worship. Why haven't we grasped the understanding that external posture is often a reflection of an internal attitude? When my heart bows in reverence to His holiness, my knees have very little difficulty following.

Responding to the Deliverer

Just as my knees bow in response to the reverence of my heart, my hands and feet can't help but respond to the power of His delivering hand. Several words describe rejoicing in God's presence and we will look at them in-depth in a later chapter. Some of them will include the concept of dance as an expression of praise and worship. This is still the most controversial of all expressions but often the most fulfilling when giving thanks for God's delivering power in our lives.

When Miriam led the worship team in a dance of celebration on the banks of the Red Sea, the song was "Sing to the Lord, for He is highly exalted; the horse and his rider He has hurled into the sea" (Exod. 15:21). Is it possible to sing that song with gusto while standing still? For those of us who have been delivered from the tyranny of Egypt's bondage, the answer is NO! It's impossible to stand with rigid arms and feet that are planted firmly in place in the presence of His awesome delivering power!

Graham Kendrick says, "A friend of mine when asked why he dances in worship of God says, 'I dance because I can't fly.'"[2] I think that sums it up! When we begin to fully appreciate the difference between the kingdoms of light and darkness, an ignition of something holy must give way to expression.

Praise: Our Acceptable Sacrifice

As a worship leader, my main responsibility is that of a gatekeeper: to lead the people into the presence of God through music. However, I'm intrigued by the ambivalent attitudes of believers who consider the praise and worship of God to be as discretionary as other activities in life: If they feel like it they will participate—sometimes wholeheartedly, sometimes not. Ben Patterson calls these "spontaneous worshipers."[3] If everything is going right for them emotionally, they "enter in."

Most Christians enter a worship gathering with an attitude of getting rather than contributing to the service. Certainly life has its ebbs and flows, but life's traumas should have no bearing whatsoever on God's worth or our responsibilities in His presence. God wants us to know that His is a house of worship, and we are responsible for how we value the worship of His presence. We are not merely to sit and drink in. We are to participate in the experience by consciously bringing a sacrifice or something of value (see Heb. 13:15). As a matter of fact, let's offer a sacrifice of praise right here:

> I praise You Lord God Almighty! You alone are worthy to be praised. I exalt the name JESUS, which is above every name. I give You glory and honor and praise.

Be Present in His Presence

I hope you benefited from speaking those words. It is possible to speak words without giving life to them. For example, have you ever driven down the road on the way to a familiar place, only to arrive and not know how you got there? Your mind was someplace else. YIKES! Thoughts of conversations with people, phone calls to return, errands to run or household chores dominated your mind. The auto-pilot mechanism in us is marvelous at times and can save our lives, if not a lot of time. Just the same, it's frightening to realize your conscious mind had nothing to do with your arrival at a specific destination.

Sometimes we can mindlessly maneuver through a worship service and not know how we did it. In the malaise of a typical Sunday morning stupor, we lose track of the motivating force behind our initiative to worship in the first place and then "wake up" 20 minutes later. The offering of praise we bring gets stuck halfway between here and Jupiter and becomes irretrievable. Besides embarrassing, this mindless activity is an insult to the majesty of God:

> "But when you present the blind [animal] for sacrifice,...the lame and the sick, is it not evil? Why not offer it to your governor? Would he be pleased with you?...You also say, 'My, how tiresome it is!' And you disdainfully sniff at it,...Should I receive that from your hand?" says the Lord (Mal. 1:8,13).

God takes worship seriously! It's not a light thing to come into His presence bearing half-hearted gifts. Some treat the sacred gathering of His people and the holy offerings of worship like a haphazard fast-food meal. They give Him the "leftovers" of their lives on the weekend instead the firstfruits of their love through the week. If we approach His majesty empty handed or with a lame sacrifice, what are the chances of gaining an audience before the throne?

In June of 1981, when Prince Charles and the late Diana were married, the media had a first-class picnic televising the event. Everyone of significance, including leaders of nations, ambassadors and dignitaries, were in attendance. Each one was seen greeting Queen Elizabeth and Prince Philip in all their regalia with a gift in their hands as they exchanged royal pleasantries before the ceremony. (I still remember Nancy Reagan's bright green dress, hat, shoes and bag.)

A lot of expensive pomp and circumstance, you may think, but a perfect picture of Proverbs 18:16: "A man's gift makes room for him, and brings him before great men." Although established millenniums ago, this ancient procedure is still practiced today. The gift, offering or sacrifice would grant a common person an audience with a nobleman or king.

What He Requires, He Provides

As the King of kings, what does God expect and require when we come into His presence? According to "the law of first mention," we pay special attention to the way a significant word is first used in Scripture. Genesis 22:5 is the first time worship is mentioned. This familiar passage is the story of Abraham and Isaac ascending Mount Moriah to present a burnt offering. As you may know, God was testing Abraham's obedience by requiring Abraham to offer his own son as a sacrifice—a perfect illustration of God offering His Son.

Isaac was aware that they had sticks and fire but he questioned the whereabouts of the lamb for the burnt offering. Like a good dad, Abraham assuaged the lad's concerns by saying, "God will provide for Himself the lamb for the burnt offering, my son" (v. 8).

I was listening to a sermon on this passage recently: "Soon enough, Isaac was informed that he was the sacrifice and to climb up on the wood. This is a parallel to the passage of Scripture from Luke 22:42 where Jesus prayed in the garden that this cup would pass from Him. Nevertheless, He said, 'Not my will but yours be done.' The Father in turn spoke to Jesus, 'Son, You are the sacrifice...climb up on the wood.'"[4]

At the point of no return, the angel of the Lord appeared to Abraham and grabbed his arm before he could slay his son. Abraham was told that his obedience was seen of God and he was instructed to spare Isaac. Then when he looked in the thicket, he found the sacrificial animal.

With a thunderous sigh of relief, Abraham took the ram and offered it to the Lord in place of Isaac. Abraham then named the place "Jehovah Jireh," meaning, "The Lord Will Provide...in the mount of the Lord it will be provided" (Gen. 22:14). Though we've looked at this Scripture and have used it to prove that God will take care of our every need, the literal meaning of this passage is, "In the place of worship, God will provide what HE requires in sacrifice."

What an awesome provision from God that even in the corporate gathering when I don't feel like giving thanks, what He requires in the sacrifice of worship, He will provide. In a very literal sense, we join the Psalmist David, saying, "From Thee comes my praise in the great assembly; I shall pay my vows before those who fear Him" (Ps. 22:25). He grants what is needed to truly worship Him.

Public rejoicing and worship is part of God's plan for us. He's destined us to be a people of praise that we may be changed as we minister to Him. As His presence is manifest in our corporate meetings, it has the inherent ability to transform our lives into His image.

Annie Dillard in her essay "Expedition to the North Pole" reflects on Christian worship and asks, "Does anyone have the foggiest idea what sort of power we so blithely invoke? The churches are children playing on the floor with their chemistry sets, mixing up a batch of TNT to kill a (beautifully planned and orchestrated) Sunday morning. It is madness to wear ladies' straw hats and velvet hats to church; we should all be wearing crash helmets. Ushers should issue life preservers and signal flares: they should lash us to our pews."[5]

Indeed! Too often we underestimate the awesome power available to us in the presence of God. The challenge is His...conforming us to the image of Christ. Let the transformation begin! Let's see Jesus!

Notes

1. Bob Sorge, *Exploring Worship* (Canandaigua, N.Y.: Oasis House Publishers, 1987), p. 37.
2. Graham Kendrick, *Learning to Worship As a Way of Life* (Minneapolis, Minn.: Bethany House Publishers, 1984), p. 15.
3. Bob Sorge, *Exploring Worship,* (quoting Ben Patterson), p. 37.
4. Paul Wilbur, *"Spirit and Truth Worship"* (Denver, Colo.; November 8, 1997).
5. Mark Galli, ed., *Mastering Worship* (Portland, Oreg.: Multnomah Press, 1990), p. 13.

Chapter Five

A Sense of Community

Blest be the tie that binds our hearts in Christian love;
The fellowship of kindred minds is like to that above.

"BLEST BE THE TIE THAT BINDS"
BY JOHN FAWCETT AND JOHANN G. NAEGLI

It was a dreary Sunday morning, and from my perch at the keyboard on the platform, the faces of the congregation resembled the hue of the sky outside—dull with shades of gray! They looked "under the weather." And yet in spite of the weather, I sensed the Lord desired a specific offering commensurate with the direction He had been leading us for several weeks. Our awareness of His faithfulness had propelled us forward as a Body to pursue the vision He had given us months prior.

When Sunday Gets Blue

We had been instructed by the Spirit of God to break down strongholds of doubt and unbelief in order to counteract the enemy's accusations against God. We were to do so by magnifying the Lord's goodness and faithfulness in our worship times. His direction was based on our need for encouragement rather than His need to see if we could succeed in the face of opposition. The breakthrough was at the door; we just needed to push it open. How trivial, it seemed, to be affected by something as volatile as the weather on this potentially eventful day. Nevertheless, though an element of grace was available, the mood of the people would deter His full purpose for the day's responsibilities.

Was God upset about our inability to rise above our circumstances? I don't think so. According to the psalmist, God understands our frame and knows that we are but dust (see Ps. 103:14). The fulfillment of His plans for us would just have to be postponed for another week. Though it was frustrating to miss an opportunity to "score" against the devil, remaining flexible with human moods and emotions is part of life and ministry.

Praise: The Power to Rise Above Our Circumstances

The variables (including the weather) on any given Sunday morning are numerous and can affect the overall flavor of a gathering. For example: Here are John and Mary (names changed) with four small children to feed, clean up and dress before walking out the door for church. What are the chances of them:

1. arriving on time;
2. with a good attitude; and
3. with hearts prepared to honor the Almighty?

Then there's Bob and Edna who have recently lost a grandchild to a rare form of cancer. Wrestling with the debilitating anguish, they're struggling to find answers to explain God's heart of love.

And what about Jackie? She's a single mom who can barely feed her three children while working two jobs. Her husband was recently incarcerated for the illegal possession and distribution of narcotics. It will be three years before their lives can attempt normalcy.

The stories of real people and the dynamics of their real-life problems can be staggering. But these people are to be commended for taking the initiative to come to a corporate worship gathering called "their church"—where they've come to know and love God and others, and be loved in spite of their flaws, hurts and lack of answers. They don't go to church to "escape" the painful reality of their lives; worshiping God is not a crutch for them. Rather, their worship is a genuine response to the pain. They choose to believe and acknowledge God as holy and righteous in all His ways—even though they may not understand His role in their present crises (see Isa. 40:31; 55:9)!

The apostle Paul said to the Thessalonian church: "In everything give thanks; for this is God's will for you in Christ Jesus" (1 Thess. 5:18). Many of us automatically sense condemnation when we read that verse. We think we're not thankful enough for the goodness of God. As true as that may be, self-condemnation never produced godly righteousness in anyone (see Rom. 8:1). If it's the kindness of God that leads us to repentance, then we must become a bit more familiar with God to discern the difference between the voice of the Spirit and our own well-hidden self-hatred.

The Grateful Heart Does Not Pretend

Scripture says, "In everything give thanks." It does not say, "*For* everything you must feel *grateful*." That would be ridiculous, if not humanly impossible. Cultivating a thankful heart is not an exercise in the mechanics of denial and disassociation. Nor is it a game of "pretend everything is OK" to avoid challenging God's faithfulness. He is much more secure than that and can handle anything that comes His way.

Psalm 97:11 says, "Light is sown like seed for the righteous, and gladness for the upright in heart." Joy in our lives is not an automatic position we achieve and maintain once we acknowledge Jesus as Lord. Joy (or light) is planted like seed in a vegetable garden. Once the seeds of joy have been planted, they must be watered and cared for until harvest time. Just when you think you've arrived at permanent contentment, you find there's more work to do on your garden of joy! The course is Thanksgiving 101.

Faith is not the absence of fear, but
your response to it!

In this course we learn lessons such as giving thanks to God because everything is NOT OK and He's the only One who can change our perspective. He's the only One who can give us wisdom for responding to our own humanity. In the midst of the most difficult experiences of life, giving thanks acknowledges Him as God and often diffuses the enemy's strategy against us.

Most of us recognize and usually desire to rise up in faith and confess things that defy reality when all along Jesus is standing nearby whispering gently, "Just come to Me. Choose to turn your focus to your heavenly Father and give thanks in spite of your dilemma. Stop pretending that everything's OK. For faith is not the absence of fear, but your response to it! You don't have to prove you're a spiritual superhero. Just focus on Me."

The Old Testament prophet responded this way:

Though the fig tree should not blossom, and there be no fruit on the vines, though the yield of the olive should fail, and the fields produce no food, though the flock should be cut off from the fold, and there be no cattle in the stalls, yet will I exult [leap about with joy] in the Lord, I will rejoice in the God of my salvation (Hab. 3:17,18).

In the face of all opposition, give thanks to the Lord. This simple act of faith, also known as "waiting upon the Lord," can renew your strength and cause you to soar above the difficulties, giving you a whole new perspective (see Isa. 40:31). God knows you need a new perspective when the old one is compelling you to throw yourself off the cliff!

It's a Matter of Focus

Perspective is a matter of focus. And as we confess Jesus as Lord, our focus follows. Richard C. Leonard states in *The Complete Library of Christian Worship*, "The phrase 'give thanks' commonly applied to worship means to 'make confession' of Yahweh as Lord and King."[1]

We sometimes confess Jesus as Lord of our lives because it's safer than saying *we* are. To make ourselves the responsible party when catastrophe strikes is paving a path to self-destruction. In moments of resignation, out of pure frustration when we randomly say, "Jesus is Lord," or, "God is in control of this situation," we have to admit to ourselves that we've lost control of the situation and hope that Jesus is watching our brave reaction to trust Him.

A Bible School instructor of mine used to say:

You never know Jesus is all you need until He's all you've got!

When we can't see light at the end of the tunnel, we must make the choice to focus on Him. We do this by choosing to praise. Praise breaks the power of negativity and fear, causing faith to rise up within us. And as faith rises, so do our eyes—looking to the One who is able to speak peace into every storm of life.

A profound illustration of the commitment to give thanks in the midst of hardship is the testimony of Horacio G. Spafford, who wrote the song "It Is Well with My Soul," originally titled "Peace Attends My Way."

Horacio Spafford, a successful businessman, and his family were Presbyterians who lost all their worldly possessions in the 1871 Chicago fire. Then in the fall of 1873 business obligations prevented Horacio from joining his wife and four daughters when they set sail on the *Ville du Havre* to vacation in France. As the mighty ocean liner charted its course through the icy waters of the Atlantic Ocean, it was struck by an English ship and sank within 12 minutes. Mrs. Spafford was among the survivors, but all four girls were lost in the wreckage of that perilous event.

Sometime later Horacio was crossing the Atlantic on his way to England when the ship's captain summoned him to the bridge. The captain pointed to the place where his four daughters had lost their lives and Horacio stepped out onto the bridge to pen these words:

When peace like a river attendeth my way,
When sorrows like sea billows roll,
Whatever my lot Thou has taught me to say,
"It is well, it is well with my soul."

He Is Our Hope

As someone once said, "When you find yourself between a rock and a hard place, remember that Jesus is the Rock." Focusing on the Rock rather than the hard place gives us a reason to praise. In hard times we can use the medium of thanksgiving and praise to overcome the pull of self-pity.

Let's try it. Will you pray with me?

Lord, though I don't understand why life is like this, I know You know the end from the beginning. I still choose to believe that You are good and worthy of praise in the midst of my current misery. Show Yourself strong for me in this situation and grace me to pursue You as my only hope. Please grant me a fresh perspective of Your

life on the other side of my present turmoil.
In Jesus' name do I trust and pray. Amen.

This kind of honesty with God allows Him to make an appearance in a situation that would otherwise seem lonely. Although Jesus said, "I WILL NEVER DESERT YOU, NOR WILL I EVER FORSAKE YOU" (Heb. 13:5), when we feel the need to "buck up" under the load of life *in our own strength*, we cut ourselves off from His divine help through others.

As Bob Sorge writes regarding the horizontal aspect of worship:

Consider first that we worship to enhance the feelings of unity within the Body of believers....We also worship in order to provide believers with an opportunity to confess and profess their faith before others.[2]

How incredibly crucial for us in these days to be afforded the privilege to confess our trust in God on a regular basis with other believers. We tend to adopt the mind-set of those with whom we keep company. Therefore, as we associate with faith-filled believers, we, too, grow in faith. Standing beside another who's "been there and done that" and can still offer praise to the name of the Lord in spite of life's troubles becomes our life-line in stormy times. We can draw strength from those whose testimony stands secure in God through the perils of living in a fallen world (see 2 Cor. 1:3,4).

Corporate Worship Promotes Unity

The Lord has planned for the corporate worship time to bring encouragement and instruction to His people as a whole body. Although the Lord will effectively deal with us as individuals, in a greater sense, His primary point in the corporate setting is to bring us together as a unit. If we are personally prepared, the extent of the Holy Spirit's ministry to us can be realized more fully.

For the last hundred years or so, it has been a common practice in some churches for the song service to precede the delivery of the Word. The idea is that we offer the sacrifice of worship to God first, then He encourages us with His Words. In some churches, however, the praise and worship part of the service is still considered to be "the preliminaries." This philosophy, based on the eighteenth-century mode of exalting the pulpit above the altar, deems the worship of God as secondary to hearing from God.

Yet the apostle Paul's suggestion points out an equally important function to the preaching of the Word in the corporate worship gathering: "Speaking to one another in psalms, hymns and spiritual songs, singing and making melody with your heart to the Lord" (Eph. 5:19).

Psalms, Hymns and Spiritual Songs

As the Church has grown in its understanding of the knowledge of God and His ways, the desire to be progressive in worship has forced many believers to throw the baby out with the bath water: in other words, to discard all traditional forms of worship for the sake of being current. And yet a quick glance at Church history shows that the Early Church used the book of Psalms as its hymnbook. The early Christians were steeped in synagogue worship, which involved the oral tradition of psalms, hymns and spiritual songs mentioned in Ephesians 5:19.

Notice that when Jesus ascended into heaven, we find the disciples filled with joy and "continually in the temple, praising God" (Luke 24:53). Praising God was part of their Davidic tradition and yet they now combined that tradition with their new-found faith in Christ. The Jewish (Old Testament) call to worship combined with a New Covenant relationship (life in Christ) brought a new sense of joy to their worship.

Psalms
The disciples understood the importance of the Psalms, which are a means of:

- Preserving God's history with His people;
- Identifying the ways to approach God;
- Learning about God's character;
- Instructing us in times of trouble;
- Encouraging our faith;
- Helping us to be real before God;
- Bringing us into the fullness of worship.

Hymns

Another avenue for the encouragement and instruction of the Body is in the use of hymns. A hymn by definition is a religious metrical composition.

Most of us are familiar to one degree or another with hymns. They are usually associated with warm memories of perhaps a childhood experience or even a funeral for a loved one. Holding Grandma's hand in church comes to mind as I think of singing the old hymns of the Church.

I remember the familiar words as we sang the song not too long ago:

My hope is built on nothing less
than Jesus' blood and righteousness.
I dare not trust the sweetest frame
but wholly lean on Jesus' name.
On Christ, The Solid Rock, I stand
All other ground is sinking sand;
All other ground is sinking sand.
("The Solid Rock" by Edward Mote and William B.
Bradbury)

The stately rendition of this traditional melody rang out. Immediately, a sense of strength and hope filled the room as the believers sang of their confidence unashamedly with this old hymn. I thought, *Can it get any better than this? At this point in time, is there a better way to encourage one anoth-*

er *toward faith in God?* Of all the confessions of faith and methods of declaring our trust in the Lord, here we were in a contemporary worship service utilizing this old hymn as a bastion of strength. I sensed a unity of "one mind and one accord" that surpassed the average worship time as we sang. It was awesome!

The use of something old and familiar took on a whole new feeling as we logged on to the network of ancient saints. The timeless experience of singing the songs of our fathers somehow puts us in touch with their historical faith.

Still, many free-praise churches have been leery of the use of historical hymns in their contemporary-styled worship services. The typical concerns range from a fear of traditionalism to the extreme of hyperemotionalism. Perhaps their reluctance is due to a lack of knowledge about how to incorporate anti-quated style without "reverting back" to antiquated attitudes. Then of course, there's always the concern of cultural relevance. We ask questions such as, Why are we doing this? Is this to demonstrate a spiritual truth, or satisfy someone's need for the old and familiar?

And yet, when Jesus once used a parable to depict some principles of the kingdom of heaven, He made the following statement:

"Therefore every scribe who has become a disciple of the kingdom of heaven is like a head of a household, who brings forth out of his treasure things *new* and *old*" (Matt. 13:52, italics added).

The useful "old" things in the treasury storehouse, those that still have life based on the relevant continuity of God's everlasting covenant, are important to the growth and progression of purpose in our congregations. The hymns of the Church that are filled with sound doctrine need to be used as teaching tools at least—better yet, as confessions of faith in the God of both history and destiny.

We cannot repent for our religious heritage, nor can we make apology for growing in grace, knowledge and understanding of God and His ways. The "faith of our fathers" is undoubtedly worth commending and gleaning from, as is the pursuit of fresh manna from God today. Truly His mercies are new every morning!

The History of Hymns

Ralph Martin from the University of Sheffield, England, says:

> Historically, the singing of hymns to deity was an established practice in the Greco-Roman world long before the emergence of Christianity. Christian hymns differed from pagan hymnody, however, in celebrating a redemptive historical event; they have "prophetic" quality.[3]

The fact that many churches still use hymns of one form or another places them in a prophetic position. Declaring the resurrection of Jesus through hymn singing is an ageless prophetic statement. Unfortunately, some hymns by their nature date themselves and are often seen as less important as long as contemporary chorus singing is preeminent. Because knowledge is increasing at such a rapid rate, song writing is also increasing. But let us never forget the great deposit of faith hymns have given·us in the pursuit of today's revelation of God!

From a historical viewpoint, the development of Christian hymns is an incredible witness to the revival of holy desire in the Church to express heartfelt worship to God in a way that was different from Latin liturgy. What began with Luther's devotional hymn writing eventually exploded into "The Golden Age of Hymns" less than 250 years ago. This relatively "new" worship phenomenon was not even officially approved in the Church of England until 1820. Yet of the 8,989 hymns contained in 56 collections by Charles and John Wesley, a good portion of those are still sung today.

Spiritual Songs

John Piper once said, "Worship is the adoration and praise of that which delights us. We praise what we enjoy, because praise completes the enjoyment. We worship God for the pleasure to be had in Him."[4]

It ought to be a pleasant experience to worship God. Unlike the worship of false gods and idols, our God favors us by allowing us pleasure as we worship Him. The sense of fulfillment in being sons of God is realized as we give honor to Him and prefer one another. Notice the simultaneous effect through this mode of offering praise. The living God is glorified and His covenant people are encouraged.

The term "spiritual song" (Greek: *Pneumatikos ode*—a supernaturally inspired or "God-breathed" melody)[5] has readily been appropriated to any kind of spontaneously sung chant or motif of spiritual origin. That is, breathed or birthed by the Spirit. The spiritual song has also become known by other names such as singing with the Spirit, the new song, the song of the Lord, the prophetic song and the selah. The use of this form of song can be demonstrated in a variety of ways in the congregation.

"Charismatic congregations frequently sing in tongues, as Paul suggests in 1 Corinthians 14:15; such singing usually follows immediately after the congregation sings in the known language....Charismatics view the vocal praise song that wells up and flows from God's people as the voice of the Spirit of God in their midst, evidence of His life being released in the sanctuary and flowing out to bless the nations."[6]

Often, a spontaneous song is lifted at a climactic point in worship which is expressed by congregational singing (in the Spirit) or in a known language (in the understanding). This new song, as it is called by many, is regularly a precursor to something further prophetic in nature. An individual may lift up his or her voice in song TO the Lord or prophetically in a song FROM the Lord. In either case, the song has its origin from the Spirit in order to edify, exhort or instruct the Body.

At times the song, sung by a solo voice, will be in the form of a love expression from the Bridegroom to the Bride. Our response to that expression ought to be our love for Him in return...because God will respond to people who respond! At other times the song may be a prayer of confession directly to God or a song exalting the name of the Lord with joy. Occasionally the song may come from the Psalms, expressing the plight of a weary soul.

For example, I remember a particular worship service when a cloud of heaviness seemed to blanket the people. I sensed by the Spirit that an extraordinary amount of discouragement and disillusionment was present that day. The feeling was not an actual blame toward God, rather a weariness with the battle of life.

As I stood at the keyboard playing softly and waiting on the Lord for direction in dealing with this foreboding presence, I turned in my Bible to Psalm 42:5 and began singing the verse spontaneously: "Why are you in despair, O my soul? And why have you become disturbed within me? Hope in God, for I shall again praise Him for the help of His presence."

Our worship creates a platform or an atmosphere in which the Holy Spirit can speak to our hearts, convicting us of sin and changing our direction.

As this Psalm depicts the psalmist speaking to his soul and not to God necessarily, one would think that we took somewhat of an "intermission" in the middle of the worship time for a little self-pep talk. Quite frankly, that's what it was. We had reached a point where we could go no further in our offering to God until our souls acknowledged their desperation and chose to agree with the purpose of the Spirit. We needed a moment to refocus our hearts and minds upon the God to whom we were singing.

After singing the Psalm through two or three times, a chorus or refrain section developed—similar to the structure of a hymn—and the congregation began singing together: "I will hope in God, I will hope in God!" Suddenly a spiritual and emotional breakthrough came. The air began to clear as we encouraged one another with this Psalm-turned-hymn, which ultimately changed into a spontaneous "spiritual song"—a strategic song that was birthed by the Spirit for that moment. The entire emotional and spiritual atmosphere was transformed, taking us to another level of trust in God.

Worship Opens Our Hearts So We Can Hear God

When we position our hearts in worship before the presence of the Almighty, He is then free to speak to us through that medium of communion. Our worship creates a platform or an atmosphere in which the Holy Spirit can speak to our hearts, convicting us of sin and changing our direction. There are many ways in which He accomplishes this. For example, the voice of God is often heard in the congregation through the administration of the gifts of the Spirit. At some point in the service in a moment of reflection after our offering of worship has been presented, someone may offer an unknown tongue and an interpretation, a word of prophecy or an exhortation by the Spirit which includes a word of knowledge or word of wisdom.

When hearts are open to receive from the Lord after presenting our offerings of worship to Him, I usually conclude that our worship time has been successful or it has "hit the mark." When Jesus is glorified, I call that success! The power of God can then rearrange our philosophy of life and godliness by infusing us with His ideals. Though the Holy Spirit may utilize the gifts of the Spirit, He never leaves out the power of His still small voice. God can speak to us quietly, personally and just as powerfully in the depths of our being without a manifestation of the vocal gifts.

Changed by the Challenge to Worship

If indeed the words of the nineteenth-century poet Thomas Carlyle are true, "Worship is transcendent wonder,"[7] then the sense of awe we experience in His presence can only lead to genuine transformation into His likeness. What could be a greater goal in this life than to be conformed to the image of Jesus? The supernatural energy available is purposed to do exactly that; change us into His likeness.

The music we sing in worship is a reflection of our hearts before God. Modern-day psalmody and hymnody could very well be fueled by the spiritual song—that which proceeds directly from the heart of God for a specific occasion. By the Spirit, this kind of worship can radically change the destiny of our expressions of praise. If we worship in the way God has prescribed with honesty of heart, the windows of heaven will open for us and the personal fulfillment we long for will be met in His presence.

Notes

1. Richard C. Leonard, *The Complete Library of Christian Worship, Vol. 1* (Nashville, Tenn.: Starsong Publishing Group, 1993), p. 3.
2. Bob Sorge, *Restoring Praise and Worship to the Church* (Shippensburg, Pa.: Revival Press, 1989), p. 38.
3. Ralph Martin, *The Complete Library of Christian Worship, Vol. 1* (Nashville, Tenn.: Starsong Publishing Group, 1993), p. 259.
4. Howard Stevenson, *Mastering Worship* (Portland, Ore.: Multnomah Press, 1990), p. 26.
5. James Strong, *Strong's Exhaustive Concordance* (Nashville, Tenn.: Crusade Bible Publishers, Inc., 1983), #5603.
6. Janice E. Leonard, *The Complete Library of Christian Worship, Vol. 1* (Nashville, Tenn.: Starsong Publishing Group, 1993), p. 274.
7. Thomas Carlyle, *On Heroes and Hero Worship*, Lecture 1 "The Hero As Divinity" (Scotland, 1841).

THAT
ALL MAY
KNOW

Oh the blood of Jesus,
Oh the blood of Jesus,
Oh the blood of Jesus,
It washes white as snow.

"OH THE BLOOD OF JESUS"
AUTHOR UNKNOWN

The words of the old familiar chorus draped like a heavenly canopy over the streets of the French Quarter in New Orleans during the Mardi Gras festival.

A group of 240 students from Christ for the Nations in Dallas, Texas, led by my friend Michael Massa, had come to the city for some intensive street ministry during the week of the nation's most debauched party. On this particular evening, the group concluded a prayer strategy meeting where the Holy Spirit instructed everyone to do nothing but worship Jesus on the streets.

There's Power in the Name and the Blood of Jesus

Hand in hand they marched down Bourbon Street, lifting their voices, exalting the name and the blood of Christ. To everyone's amazement, the streets were relatively quiet and uneventful that night. In obedience they marched, lifting up Jesus. Then suddenly several young people came running through the crowd, each one begging, "I want what you have! Tell me more about Jesus!"

Coincidentally, no violence erupted on Bourbon Street that night, while virtually all hell broke loose several blocks away with some serious fighting and even a gunshot murder. It was as if the protective blood of Jesus were flooding out demonic forces to some outer limits.

The impact of the event still moves me today as I reflect on the power of worship to the unbeliever—especially outside the four walls of the church building. I was amazed to see the authority of the name of Jesus in action. As Scripture says, demons tremble at the sound of His name (see Mark 16:17). If we could only fully comprehend the power in His name, we would probably be more open to sharing the gospel (see John 14:14; Acts 4:12,30; Phil. 2:9,10). Spiritual things are not seen with the natural eye, therefore, they usually translate into a nonchalant approach to faith-filled actions. If we knew what our worship was accomplishing in the spirit world, we'd probably be more diligent in the pursuit of the heathen.

If the People Won't Go to the Church, the Church Must Go to the People

Street ministry has proven to be a valid form of evangelism throughout the years, even though the Church's usual expectation is that the unbeliever must come to our worship services to meet Jesus. Jesus' ministry was in sharing meals with publicans and sinners on their turf. He took the truth of His life to them!

Jesus' Great Commission to make disciples of all the nations (see Matt. 28:18-20) is still binding on Christians today, although our methods of outreach have changed or been modified over the centuries. No matter what their culture or background, people need the Lord, so whatever means used to share the living gospel is worthy of consideration. Worship is a means for drawing people of every culture into the Kingdom. The following is a story from Cindy Jacobs's book *Possessing the Gates of the Enemy*, exemplifying the power of praise on the streets:

> Shiloh Christian Fellowship had always been known as a worshiping church, and the members believed earnestly in the power of worship to bind the enemy. They did not realize how much the word had gotten around about their worship until one day they received an invitation from the Oakland Police Department. Would they be willing to go to Pleitner Avenue and see what could be done for the area? Pleitner Avenue at the time was infested with drug lords, pimps and prostitutes, a rough, dangerous part of Oakland.
>
> After they got over their surprise at the invitation, they said they would be glad to go. As they prayed they devised a plan. Working with the police they marked off an area of the street to have a block party. They planned to give away clothes, cook hot dogs, worship God according to Psalm 149 and then preach an evangelistic message. The church went back for three Saturdays in a row. The results were incredible. In fact, the police told the media about the parties and reported the results in the newspaper. According to the police reports, 70 percent of the drug lords moved out of the Pleitner Avenue area after the parties.[1]

Here was a group of people taking the authority of the name of Jesus into the depths of a hell-infested neighborhood to loosen Satan's hold. What they had learned about the power of praise and worship was being exhibited in one of the darkest areas of town. Not only was Jesus glorified in the spiritual realm, but He also became glorified on the earth through His people. The spiritual effects were evidenced in the natural realm. Talk about intensive street ministry—this was the height of a serious assault on the kingdom of darkness as the unique qualities inherent in the praise of God were demonstrated boldly on the streets.

Graham Kendrick, noted for his pioneering work with praise marches on the streets of London and the International Marches for Jesus, was speaking to a group of worship leaders in Dallas, Texas. Introducing the concept of the March, he said, "People are not brought into the Kingdom by mere miracles alone. Jesus did miracles, then they killed Him. They need a spiritual encounter with God."[2]

Praise: The Calling Card of Heaven

As a participant in several of the Marches throughout the past few years, I've noticed that the onlookers—though overwhelmed by the number of people brave enough to profess Jesus on the streets of the city—were captivated by the praise of Jesus' name. Many unbelievers have come into the Kingdom by experiencing the presence of God through these Marches. It's a graphic illustration of Jesus being lifted up and drawing all men to Himself (see John 12:32).

When the unsaved world *sees* the relationship we have in worshiping the only true and living God, it is intrigued. Our praise diffuses negativity and floods the environs with hope and life. We then become salt and light, pointing those who do not know Him to the Savior.

I was recently told of a short-term missions outreach to Guatemala that graphically illustrates this point. My pastor's wife, Ceci Sheets, was with a group of young people ministering in a Guatemalan hospital. The leader of the group instructed everyone with the team to worship in song. Timidly they began to sing. The leader fervently prodded them to increase their volume and intensity. As they engaged their hearts in song, a confident faith permeated the atmosphere. Worship began to ascend in this large dormlike room while the sick and diseased listened and felt the presence of God.

Suddenly a voice rung out from across the room shouting, "Milagro! Milagro!" (meaning Miracle! Miracle!). Running to see what the commotion was all about, several from the team found a screaming woman—who had been crippled in all extremities from a doctor's mistake during surgery—stretching out her arms, legs, fingers and toes. God had instantly healed her!

This healing was quite an unexpected occurrence. Other patients in the large room immediately began clamoring for prayer. Many people were healed and gave their lives to Jesus that day—the result of a brief worship gathering in a Guatemalan hospital.

True Praise Transforms the Heart and Causes the Hands and Feet to Obey

Psalm 40:1-3 explains how praise transforms us and causes us to draw attention to the Lord:

> I waited patiently for the Lord; and He inclined to me, and heard my cry. He brought me up out of the pit of destruction, out of the miry clay; and He set my feet upon a rock making my footsteps firm. And He put a new song in my mouth, a song of praise to our God; many will see and fear, and will trust in the Lord.

I read an article in which a prominent worship leader shared the following encounter with the late Mother Teresa in India:

> She said that when she helped on orphan in the street or when she gave a cup of cold water to a thirsty child, she was worshiping God. "After all," she challenged him,

"didn't Jesus say whatever you did for the least of these brothers of mine, you did for me?" (Matt. 25:40).[3]

The "new song" in Mother Teresa's mouth produced an attractive behavior that drew people to her. Her actions literally became the hands and feet of the Master, reaching out to the oppressed and needy in the worst of life's situations. For this woman, who represented the epitome of selfless giving, worship entailed a much broader scope than being confined to a congregation. Paying tribute to the principles of Jesus' loving care was paramount to her existence.

Thus, we see that worship is more than just a melodic song. The song merely gives words to the overflow of the heart. And a heart that truly worships is evidenced by a life that is surrendered to His service. Honoring God by giving to others less fortunate is one of the cardinal truths of "pure religion":

This is pure and undefiled religion in the sight of our God and Father, to visit orphans and widows in their distress, and to keep oneself unstained by the world (Jas. 1:27).

Exalting Jesus takes on a number of forms, many of which we would consider "Christian activities." Good deeds though they may be—only when the world sees our love for the Lord being demonstrated in genuine care for humanity does true worship occur...where God is preeminent and the focus of attention.

Bigger Than a Building, But Not Too Big for a Human Heart

Although seeing the power of worship outside the four walls of the church building is a novelty, another avenue in which the unbeliever may encounter God is in congregational worship. When the life of the Spirit is demonstrated through worship, the relationship we have with this supernatural power causes the internal natural worship instinct to rise to the surface. The reason worship "works" so well on the streets is because it is something that cannot be contained or packaged. The religious stigma of "church" isn't present, which gives God the opportunity to prove He is much bigger than a building or institution.

Perhaps you've heard some nineteenth-century revival stories of people passing by a church building and being drawn inside after hearing the sounds of worship. My friend Kay Hiramine told me about a worship service at Latter Rain Church in Kuala Lumpur, Malaysia, where this kind of experience happened.

The congregation was meeting for worship on the third floor of a downtown building. A passerby heard the music and worship wafting down the stairwell and was overcome by the drawing of a supernatural presence. The man sprinted up the stairs to the meeting room and fell on his face under the conviction of the Holy Spirit. Crying out for mercy, he received an impartation of the holy life of God through a worship experience.

Just as it was when Isaiah saw the Lord, the first thing he said was, "Woe is me, for I am ruined! Because I am a man of unclean lips" (Isa. 6:5). Meeting God face-to-face in that dimension, a man finds himself forced into realizing his internal condition—wretched and poor, blind and naked without Him (see Rev. 3:17). When he confesses that truth and does not hide from it, God meets him in that place of honesty and offers a life-transforming encounter. The realization of God's mercy opens the door wide for him to join with others in giving thanks to God. The dirge of death then turns into a dance of deliverance.

We Overcome Through the Word of Our Testimony

The testimony of God's freedom when expressed in corporate worship carries a weight of prophetic significance. Our proclamation of the life of God in us produces a reaction in both those who believe and those who don't. We *must* declare our deliverance from sin and bondage to the things of this world. We *must* confess that our life and trust is in God and not in the establishments of men. We *must* profess that Jesus is the ONLY way to the Father. These are the fundamental truths of God's Word and His holy Church which are to be proclaimed in the face of the world's vehement opposition. If the believers don't become His spokespeople, who will?

> Let the redeemed of the Lord say so, whom He has redeemed from the hand of the adversary (Ps. 107:2).

What the psalmist is trying to communicate is our need to testify of God's goodness. If you have been redeemed from the hand of the enemy, then you must confess with your mouth the simple truth that Jesus has set you free! This is for you and for others. As the old hymn states, "Redeemed, how I love to proclaim it. Redeemed by the blood of the Lamb...." I've been purchased back by Jesus' life's blood. Let it be known to all!

The psalmist David prayed, "Teach me Thy way, O Lord; I will walk in Thy truth; unite my heart to fear Thy name....For Thy lovingkindness toward me is great, and Thou hast delivered my soul from the depths of Sheol" (Ps. 86:11,13). His prayer for the fear of the Lord was accompanied by a testimony of God's past deliverance and faithfulness. Let us never forget where He brought us from. Though we are not to dwell on the things of the past, deliverance from the oppression of Egypt's prison can never be forgotten. The memory of its tyranny is the springboard from which we launch into a fulfilled life of thanksgiving and heartfelt worship. He brought us out of bondage to lead us into freedom!

Will you take a moment right now to list some of the things God has done for you? As you consider His compassion toward you, just begin to speak out your appreciation. Allow your thanks to become an offering to Him. You might even want to sing a prayer from your heart right now.

When His Name Is Exalted, People Respond in Worship

I remember the days of the good old fashioned testimony services where people stood up and gave glory to God for His victories in their lives. The denomination in which I was raised used testimonials as a practical part of every service. The testimonies ranged in gratefulness from, "Jesus saves me and keeps me," to, "I used to be a rebel, but now...." Those confession times of life in Christ were very encouraging to me. Unfortunately, in many circles, they increasingly digressed from the purpose of encouraging the Body to grim group therapy sessions for those needing someone to listen to their problems.

Still, the power of one's testimony as spoken or sung in the midst of the congregation has a twofold purpose:

1. Edification of self and others;
2. Witness of God's reality to unbelievers.

In corporate worship, either in the sanctuary or on the street, the unbeliever is pointed to the Lord as the "song (or hymn) of praise" is lifted to the Lord. This praise word, *tehillah* in Hebrew, is the same word that is used in Psalm 22:3 when the psalmist says, "O Thou who art enthroned upon the praises of Israel."[4] This is the kind of praise that the Lord "inhabits"; the praise that testifies of God's deliverance from sin and death.

Please understand this is not only a song that is raised, but also a living witness of God's activity in someone's life. It is a behavioral pattern that is established in a life that has experienced the contrasting reality of spiritual death and life!

According to various other Hebrew words for praise, clearly God does not abide, inhabit, ride upon or enthrone Himself on just any kind of praise—His habitation is in praise that first recognizes *His holiness*. To recognize and revere His holiness is to also acknowledge His power to deliver from death. God's ability to redeem and set free is often realized simultaneously when His holiness is revealed. This would lend credence to the Mardi Gras story I mentioned at the beginning of this chapter. The Lord was abiding in those praises and made Himself real to a number of unbelievers as the worship of His name created a habitation for Him.

In His Presence

When the Temple was dedicated, Solomon prayed, "So now arise, O Lord God, and come into Your resting place, You and the ark of Your strength and power. Let Your priests, O Lord God, be clothed with salvation, and let Your saints (Your zealous ones) rejoice in good and in Your goodness" (2 Chron. 6:41, *Amp.*). After Solomon invited the Lord to move into His new resting place, the glory of the Lord so filled the house that the priests could not minister while standing. They could do nothing but fall down in reverence to the majesty of His awesome presence.

When the weight of God's presence rests in His house, we, too, must attempt to do nothing other than wait on Him while His glory fills the house. When the Holy Spirit makes an appearance, He usually has an agenda. First, however, we must take time to acknowledge His presence. We must always make room for the Lord to rest with us and bring rest to us. After we have welcomed His presence and entered into His rest, then we are ready to engage in those things He is calling us to do.

Occasionally the Holy Spirit directs us to war against demonic or soulish strongholds that have exalted themselves above the knowledge of God. These are often subtle accusations against the faithfulness or character of God that thrive in some hearts. Both believer and unbeliever alike have a propensity toward doubt and unbelief on any given day. This lack of faith could be due to some unresolved personal issue with God or another person, or just with life in general. These feelings leave people vulnerable to suggestions from all sides. Often, their only recourse is to adopt a skeptical view of God's presence and dealings as well as His love. The responsibility of the Body in this case is to strengthen the feeble knees and lift up the hands that hang down (see Heb. 12:12).

When we act as if our God is the biggest,
He's empowered by our faith to show Himself
to those who don't think so.

Eventually, God's wrath is exercised against these accusations of His holiness, and judgment will come in a variety of ways as the Lord's anger burns against the non-flesh-and-blood opposition. Sometimes the enemy tries to interfere in worship by creating diversions in people's minds. During those moments, the believers' sensitivity to the Holy Spirit is crucial for those whose lives hang in the balance. As the presence of God hovers over us, we the Church must "carry" the weaker among us in intercession. This can be done simply by exalting the name and authority of Jesus over every other name.

Breaking the Strongholds of Corporate Worship

Of the six fundamental feelings in the spectrum of human emotion—mad, sad, glad, fear, pain and shame—strongholds of darkness can take up residence in those areas of "feeling" and rule an individual's emotions. The representation of a host of names can be found in any given service such as pride, anger, mistrust, doubt, unbelief, false happiness...(and a hundred more). We can choose to say, "This battle is too much to handle," or we can say, "Jesus is greater than all that!" and watch Him move in partnership with our faith.

If the Holy Spirit's plan is to show us the heart of God in corporate worship, then it's reasonable to assume that He's always reaching out to the unbeliever and the weak of heart. When we act as if our God is the biggest, He's empowered by our faith to show Himself to those who don't think so.

Many believe Lucifer was once the worship leader of heaven, which explains his hatred for the praise of God. He understands the power released in worship. Ruling over regions, territories and nations with his host of fallen angels while blinding the eyes of humanity to the gospel has been a favorite pastime he's not willing to relinquish easily. So, if he can distract us from our primary objective of exalting Jesus above every name, he continues to win over God's people and maintains his death grip on the unbeliever.

The Holy Spirit Releases Truth

When the Spirit of God is present in a gathering, He "comforts the afflicted and afflicts the comfortable." That about sums up the work of the Holy Spirit. His occupational record proves His focus of ministry is to convict people of sin, to point us to Jesus as the Redeemer and to impart His holiness that we may live in (not just visit sporadically) the presence of God. As He imparts truth, the enabling qualities of God's presence prepare us for some of the "greater things than these" that Jesus talked about in John 14:12. This promise is for those who have an operating knowledge of God and His ways, which can only be learned by being with Him.

To know God, in the deepest sense of the Hebrew word *yada´*, as we discussed earlier, is to be intimate with; very much like the intimacy shared between a husband and wife in marriage. Both the physical union and the exchange of heart-to-heart communication is pictured in this word. Knowing God is the fundamental essence of real life which is sustained through an open and honest relationship with Him (see Ps. 15:1,2).

Daniel 11:32 says, "but the people who know their God will display strength and take action." Though we've used this Scripture to support a plethora of noble and sometimes militant Christian activities, this entire passage is in reference to preserving the Temple and the true worship of God. He is saying here that those who are intimate with God will be strengthened and zealous for Him and will take action to maintain the integrity of His purpose in His house.

Caring for the Father's House

As the prodigals return, the Father's House represents restored sonship and authority—a reestablished love relationship that grants fresh vision of the Father's intention for His family. When we embrace the purpose and function of His house, He will impart holy zeal and jealousy for its integrity.

Ideally, the many facets and functions of the Father's family are the spawn of their relationship with one another. Initiated by the head of the household, the chores each one assumes are for the benefit and comfort of the entire family. For example, as a father, I try to keep the household chores interesting and exciting by building into my children an appreciation for one another. I let them know that the personal chores assigned are meant to bless each other—not wreck their lives. Like most of us, sometimes they moan and complain, hoping that someone will take pity on them and excuse them from their drudgery. If I excuse them, however, they won't learn the value of simple disciplines that will definitely bless their future lives. And when they realize that their personal responsibilities affect the "flow" of unity and harmony among the family, they tend to approach their duties with a better attitude.

Keeping the family analogy in mind, God's house is designed to function similarly. There are a number of "chores" that must be performed to maintain the health of His family. When we understand these chores and the effect our part plays in the overall scheme of things, we can approach our responsibilities with a sense of valuable participation, regardless of whether or not it "feels good" to us. Following Father's agenda for the house will keep us from tailoring our own and wanting to put His name on it.

The Father's House: A House of Prayer and Praise

The result of this zeal for God's house is the same as Jesus had in Matthew 21:13. While driving out the moneychangers He said, "It is written, 'My house shall be called a house of prayer'; but you are making it a robbers' den." God intended that His house be "a house of prayer for all the peoples" (Isa. 56:7). Oh, that God would find us with such consuming zeal for His house that in the midst of our worship we would recognize our responsibilities as family members and be empowered to take action in prayer for the nations of the earth.

The marriage of prayer and praise is described through this passage in Isaiah 56:7: "My house shall be called a house of prayer." The words "of prayer" (*tephillah* in Hebrew) communicate a prayer that is set to music and sung in formal worship. *Tephillah* actually means an intercessory song and appears 77 times in the Old Testament.[5] This verse could read: "My house will be called a house of prayer and praise."

From the beginning, as ancient language provides clear reference to the purpose of the covenant, God's heart has been toward the nations of the earth. As Creator of all, it would be absurd for Him to abdicate His right to all the nations but Israel. If "the earth is the Lord's, and all it contains" (Ps. 24:1), all things are obviously His. One would assume then that His intention is to keep it that way. The nations of the earth belong to God and His family has been commissioned to secure them as their joint inheritance with Jesus.

God's plan to give the nations to Jesus as an inheritance can be heard in the words of the obscure Old Testament prophet: "'In that day I will raise up the fallen booth [Tabernacle] of David, and wall up its breaches; I will also raise up its ruins, and rebuild it as in the days of old; that they may possess the remnant of Edom and all the nations [or Gentiles] who are called by My name,' declares the Lord who does this" (Amos 9:11,12; see also Ps. 2:8).

The Tabernacle of David was an Old Covenant picture of free access to the Holy Place. Intimate fellowship with God was experienced through spontaneous worship, and then a manifestation of His presence would follow. God's prophetic purpose in "restoring" David's Tabernacle in the end times (see Amos 9:11,12; Acts 7:46; 15:16) was for all the nations to know His covenant and be welcomed into His family. God wanted to show Himself to all the peoples, using Israel as a prototype of covenantal relationship.

This place of worship could be seen as a commissioning center for God's people to possess the nations. God's promise to restore both the worship of His name and His people's inheritance comes through loud and clear. This "restoration" of the Tabernacle began when Jesus the Messiah was born, pointing the way to God. His ministry of "holy mapping" for all peoples continues today through His covenant believers.

Rebuilding the Tabernacle Through Worship

One way in which this Tabernacle is "rebuilt" today is through regular gatherings of worship. Our prescribed ceremony begins with using the blood of Christ to enter the Holy Place. This precedes intimate fellowship with God and is followed by a manifestation of His presence. As in David's day, there is freedom to minister to the Lord and hear His voice for the things on His heart. This is where some of our "chores" fit into the service of the sanctuary.

As we lift up the name of the Lord in worship, it is fitting to offer prayers and petitions for the nations of the earth. Sensitivity to the move of the Spirit will reveal how we should intercede for the things on God's heart. By the Spirit we can hear what is pressing on God's agenda at the moment. Perhaps there's an ethnic group ready for harvest and we need to pray for laborers to be commissioned. Or maybe there's a civil war about to erupt in some remote area of the world that will impede the progress of the gospel....In any case, it is possible to access God's agenda through the exaltation of His name (see Ps. 22).

Combined with our "Hallelujahs" and praises to God, we lift up cries of "Hosanna," "Have mercy, Lord. Save NOW!" The biblical precedent for this, found in Psalm 118, shows that in the midst of festive celebration and sacrifice, there is a cry from God's people for mercy and salvation. We worship not only to exalt the name of God but also to implore His saving grace in situations needing divine intervention.

A perfect illustration of this was recently performed by New Life Church in Colorado Springs. My friend and fellow worship leader Ross Parsley produced a recording project that captured the essence of worship and intercession for the nations. The project, entitled "Shine Your Light Through the Window," was initially designed to create an awareness of praying for the nations in the 10/40 Window. Woven into the song of worship by Lynn DeShazo, "The People on Your Heart," were prayers by various international Christian leaders who petitioned the Lord for receptivity to the gospel and spiritual awakening in foreign lands. As they sang and prayed, a beautiful picture was manifested of the marriage between "Hallelujah" and "Hosanna."

The true worship of God puts us in touch with the eternal value system of heaven. People from every tribe and tongue around the throne are a consistent reminder of God's heart for the kingdoms of the earth. When we accept our responsibilities in His presence, worship and intercession become companions. "Behold, bless the Lord, all servants of the Lord, who serve [or watch] by night in the house of the Lord!" (Ps. 134:1). The instruction in this verse is to the watchman or intercessor. Worship as you watch and stand in the gap....Praise while you pray....Offer thanks while you intercede.

Another passage of Scripture that points to the dual purpose of the worshiper and intercessor is in the revelation of John: "And when He had taken the book, the four living creatures and the twenty-four elders fell down before the Lamb, having each one a harp, and golden bowls full of incense, which are the prayers of the saints" (Rev. 5:8).

The elders in heaven have in their possession a harp and a bowl. The harp represents worship and the golden bowl of incense represents the prayers and intercessions of God's people on the earth. With those items in hand, they sing a new song: "Worthy art Thou to take the book, and to break its seals" (v. 9). From a position of worship and prayer, they acknowledge the Lamb's worth to answer those prayers by pouring out His righteous judgments.

As we worship and intercede for people and nations, we, as God's vehicle and channel in the earth who stand in the gap, release Him to act. The elders in heaven await our cooperation before handing the vials of prayers to angelic messengers for delivery of the judgments of God. And because God is looking for a people to pray His will, our doing so, combined with thanksgiving, releases Him to do His will.

Songs of praise and worship in the sanctuary prepare the way for further acts of the Spirit. As we've already discussed in the last chapter, various "chores of the Church" in worship are conducive to the growth of the Body and should be viewed as opportunities for joyful, zealous service. Intercession through worship is but another method of maturing a fellowship to look outside of its personal arena into the eternal realm where God lives. The way He sees things is a liberating breath of fresh air in our often stale mode of personal need. When the Spirit moves us to intercession in worship, we partake of the awesome privilege to be used of God to affect the destinies of men and nations through our worship.

The point of this kind of intercessory worship is that we bring the "remnants of the peoples" of the earth before the throne of God—the ultimate resting place of every redeemed nation, tribe, kindred and tongue—as the Scripture says, "All the earth will worship Thee, And will sing praises to Thee" (Ps. 66:4). With eternity in mind, this is true prophetic preparation for the climactic destiny of global worship in heaven.

Several years ago Laurie and I organized an international worship team in Korea for the "Gideon's Army" meeting. Three hundred intercessors from around the world were invited to participate in a prayer and intercession gathering that preceded the General Council on World Evangelization (GCOWE). One evening during worship as we sang, "Your Kingdom shall reign over all the earth," an incredible surge of power blew into the room. There we were, standing together in worship with people from scores of nations. This was a prophetic foretaste of world-wide revival as well as eternal destiny.

Saying What the Father Says

I saw yet another "chore" of the Church that coincides with intercessory worship. Many Christian prognosticators have alluded to this current renewal and revival as preparation for a "last days harvest." If indeed that is so, we must take seriously our role in the pursuit of the fruit. We must first believe that God did not make a mistake in His predestination of us in this century. He has us in His plan on purpose to act as vessels of His glory and judgment. Therefore we must begin functioning with a more thorough understanding of our present job description.

We are on the earth for a number of reasons—one of which is to continue speaking the truth of His life and kingdom. This is one aspect of Christianity that distinguishes us from any fanatical group who exalts their gods—we have a "covenantal prophetic edge." To hear God's voice and to speak God's words in the midst of a perverse and decadent society is nothing short of preposterous, and lunacy to the world's way of thinking. Just as it was in Noah's day, we as His people have a commission to declare the truth. When we accept this as another "household chore" in the congregation of the saints, it is called prophetic worship. What God is saying in heaven, we hear and declare on the earth. As Jesus prayed, "Thy kingdom come. Thy will be done, on earth as it is in heaven" (Matt. 6:10).

With so many teachings on the Lord's prayer, here's a contemporary rendition of this passage that the Church is beginning to embrace as a potential twenty-first century motto: "Kingdom of God, COME! Will of God, BE DONE!

Notes

1. Cindy Jacobs, *Possessing the Gates of the Enemy* (Grand Rapids: Chosen Books, 1991), pp. 175-176.
2. Graham Kendrick, "Introducing the March for Jesus" (Dallas, Tex.: July 1991, address to worship leaders).
3. Gerrit Gustafson as quoted by Tom Kraeuter, "Worship, a Way of Life" (*Morning Star Journal*, Vol. 8, No. 1), p. 61.
4. James Strong, *Strong's Exhaustive Concordance* (Nashville, Tenn.: Crusade Bible Publishers, Inc., 1983), #8416.
5. Ibid., #8605.

THE PROPHETIC EDGE

We see Jesus seated at the right hand of the throne,
Making intercession for His own
Upholding all things by His Word alone.
For You are glorious, shining victorious o'er powers
and principalities.
For You are glorious, shining victorious, disarming
all Your enemies.
The rulers of this world beneath Your feet are
hurled
As You reign our conquering King.

"FOR YOU ARE GLORIOUS"
BY DAVID MORRIS AND MIKE MASSA, 1988 INTEGRITY'S
HOSANNA MUSIC

Psalms, hymns and spiritual songs in the corporate setting are integral parts of our worship experience that create a sense of belonging. They remind us that we are not alone in our own personal foxholes, fighting unseen evil forces tooth and nail. Rather we are part of a broader spectrum of people who put their trust in an awesome God in response to their weaknesses. With that in mind, the voice of the Lord motivates us in the battle through songs of faith and courage in His ever-capable leadership.

I can see the Commander in Chief Himself riding out on a white horse, confidently leading the entourage of triumphal saints into victory. What a magnificent picture of the overwhelming conquest gained over the enemies of His cross! This is not only a symbolic and prophetic illustration of things to come, but also a current representation of what transpires when God's people take their role as prophetic worshipers.

The plethora of discussion and teaching about the merit of the spiritual song and the "prophetic" these days brings with it a myriad of mental images. When we hear the word "prophetic," we usually think of an individual who alone delivers the foretelling "Word of the Lord" to us personally or to the congregation. There are those who operate in the gift of prophecy as well as those who are prophets. With both, the Holy Spirit moves upon the individual by inspiration to speak God's words.

Not All Prophetic Worship Is the Same

Whenever the term "prophetic" is mentioned in relation to music and worship, however, be assured it means different things to different people. The definitions range from personal prewritten songs of edification, to churchwide exhortations with spontaneous flare. In any case, the song of the Lord or the prophetic song is found operating in many congregations today as the sounds of renewal sweep across the people of God. God is singing over His people again and the refreshing is real!

As the Lord is restoring the offices of the apostle and the prophet in our day, the proper inclination is to look to those who function in these ministry gifts to provide vision in God's house and offer spiritual guidance for God's people. Typically we view these leaders as those with the "Word of the Lord" for a local congregation or individual.

I often ask groups of people what they feel the "current Word of the Lord" is for the Body of Christ. Responses vary from "repentance and holiness," to, "joy and renewal." There are no wrong answers to that question provided we give some thought to what He is saying. If I were to boil down all those good answers into one, perhaps it could be said this way: God is ready for His Bride (the Church) to get her act together so He can fully use her to accomplish His purposes on the earth.

Although God's current words to us sometimes come through the voice of the prophet, His desire is that all His people would be channels of His divine voice on the earth. As valid and important as these individual modern-day prophets are, there is an incredible untapped well of prophetic impetus present in every one of our worship services when we gather in Jesus' name.

Oracles of Blessing and Judgment

Biblically and historically when the Lord has "shown up" in time and history, His purpose has been to pronounce blessing on the righteous and judgment on the wicked. The fundamental and prevailing understanding of God is that He is pleased with those who obey and displeased with those who don't! As a prophetic people, we function as a vehicle for these verdicts of God to be rendered.

We, the people of God, have the privilege of acting as coworkers with Him in the pursuit of reclaiming His possession and inheritance. We accomplish this through our worship of Him as the owner. Congregational worship then assumes another household chore of informing spiritual principalities that the authority of the Resurrection is far greater than any other event in history. What could be more powerful than proclaiming the power of the Cross over the power of sin and death?

When Praise Is Offensive

While reading from Psalm 149:6: "Let the high praises of God be in their mouth, and a two-edged sword in their hand...," I have wondered, *What are these "high praises" and for what purpose are they to be raised? What is this sword and what's it doing in* our hand? What's the connection between human praise and divine judgment?

To a large degree, the following verses make it clear that there is an offensive function to the praise of God combined with His Word:

> To execute vengeance on the nations, and punishment on the peoples; to bind their kings with chains, and their nobles with fetters of iron; to execute on them the judgment written; This is an honor for all His godly ones. [So, go ahead and...] Praise the Lord! (Ps. 149:7-9).

Though this concept may be a bit difficult to understand, there is undoubtedly a spiritual correlation between the praise of God and the punishment of God's enemies. Whatever the precise connection is between worship and spiritual warfare, the Lord wants us to be aware of these principles to further the impact of punishment against evil forces.

The Hebrew words used for "praise" in Psalm 149:6 and "prayer" in Isaiah 56:7 are closely related. "Praise" is *tehillah*.[1] "Prayer" is *tephillah*.[2] These two words appear to be interrelated as prophetic songs and prophetic prayers. When we allow the prophetic song to be in our mouth, God inhabits that kind of praise. With God present, no wonder principalities and powers are defeated and bound up as these high praises are offered.

The offensive power of praise is clearly illustrated by the children of Israel under Joshua's leadership, who after walking around the walls of Jericho quietly for six days, only had to raise a loud shout of praise on the seventh day. Following those simple instructions, they saw the hand of God destroy the walls of the city and then were able to conquer it.

Rhetorically, my question is, Was the shout against the enemy, or was it a vocal "Amen" to the judgment of God? In one sense, regardless of what the answer is, the fact remains that the walls came-a-tumblin'-down. God made His point well when He showed up in the shout!

We've heard a lot about the glory of the Lord in His manifest presence. We pray about it and sing about it, often begging God to show us His glory. Due to the transforming power we've experienced before in worship, we've come to know that the

> *We, as part of His army, have the honor of lifting up praise to His name and watching it defeat powers of darkness.*

energy of His presence is what makes all the difference in our often ordinary and mundane lives. There is an aspect of His presence that is violent toward the enemy and includes the principle of warfare. Dr. David Blomgren, author of *Restoring Praise and Worship to the Church*, shares his insight concerning this idea:

> This is illustrated in Numbers 4:23 where the Lord is speaking to Moses about those who are appointed to be priests. He described them as all those who "enter in to perform the service...." The words, "perform the service" are from Hebrew words which mean, literally, "fight the warfare." "Perform" is the translation of the Hebrew word *tsaba*, from which we get *sabbaoth* or hosts—as in Lord of Hosts, a name with strong military overtones...the priests entered into the holy place to fight a warfare.[3]

To bless the Lord of Hosts in the performance of a service of worship is to invoke His wrath over His enemies. We, as part of His army, have the honor of lifting up praise to His name and watching it defeat powers of darkness. We see results in the natural realm when battles are first fought in the spiritual realm.

I find the story of Jehoshaphat's army being led by the musicians and the choir to be one of the most intriguing in the Bible. The armies of Judah were surrounded by enemy troops, which caused King Jehoshaphat to seek the Lord. God, in His desire to show Himself strong, gave the king both encouragement and clear instruction. He told Jehoshaphat, "You need not fight in this battle; station yourselves, stand and see the salvation of the Lord on your behalf, O Judah and Jerusalem. Do not fear or be dismayed; tomorrow go out and face them, for the Lord is with you" (2 Chron. 20:17).

So the king rounded up the worship team and told them to precede the army in battle the next morning. (This was definitely no picnic for those musicians and far from a therapeutic assignment to simply build their faith. What could he have been thinking?)

There would be no fighting that day as the Lord would do so for them, just as He said. To prove his trust in God, King Jehoshaphat dispatched a group of unarmed worshipers to prepare the way for the Lord. As they sang and praised the beauty of holiness, the Lord took the worship of His name and used it as a paved road for His judgment to descend upon. He then set ambushments against Judah's enemies. The victory was so incredibly overwhelming, the enemy forces turned on themselves and destroyed one another.

Praise: A Tool for Exaltation or a Weapon of Warfare?

So is our praise directed to God or against the enemy? Do we confess the Lordship of Jesus Christ or our victory over darkness? Is He the object of our worship or the means to greater dimensions of authority? I don't believe the answers are either/or, but a hearty YES! The simultaneous accomplishment of exaltation and battle occurs in the primary elements of praise lifted to God. Consider the following:

> As the multitudes of heaven sang and worshiped the Lamb, The Holy One issued forth decrees against His enemies. As His words hit the target, accomplishing their purpose, the song swelled to a thunderous crescendo that shook the walls of the heavenly temple. The celestial hosts rejoiced with a loud noise in the righteousness of His judgments as once again the words of God were carried by messengers of brilliant light and poured out upon His demonic adversaries.

This almost sounds like it could be an excerpt from a Frank Perretti book. Actually, it's a paraphrase of the first half of Revelation 19 where the multitudes of heaven are rejoicing in the way God pronounces judgment.

Have you ever rejoiced because God vindicated you in a personal situation? I'm certain we all have. It's wonderful to know that God's verdict of judgment on our behalf is filled with great mercy toward us and great wrath toward our enemies. But how about something less personal but much larger in scale and broader in scope, such as a national socioeconomic situation?

For example, several years ago a particular supreme court judge who readily suppressed many Christian causes finally died. The Body of Christ was in many respects stunned by the event and didn't know how to respond. Some with mercenary madness smugly said, "It's about time. Praise God he's dead!" Others in reposed resignation said, "May the will of God be done. Lord have mercy."

What about the recent death of Anton Levay, founder of the Church of Satan? Consider what the *Church's* reaction should be to this finale. Then consider what *God's* divine will in a situation such as this would be. This goes far beyond the apostle's instruction to simply "give thanks in all things." Once again we must look at heaven's model for an appropriate response to a judgment from God that is manifest in the earth.

The apostle John deals with this directly in Revelation 19. The great multitude in heaven is heard crying out with a loud voice in praise to God because He judged the great harlot who was corrupting the earth with her immoralities. (I believe the great harlot was a political and religious institution that was responsible for the blood of the martyrs.)

According to this writing, God sent swift, definite and complete judgment to her on the earth for her corruption as the cloud of witnesses in heaven rejoiced in the righteous way God rendered those judgments. This passage of Scripture, which is also known as the Fourfold Hallelujah, includes the marriage supper of the Lamb as the final act of covenantal consummation after God's enemies are judged.

The Body of Christ is an integral part of the heavenly scheme as God's vehicle for justice in the earth. Again, to say that God has need of anything is absurd, but He has chosen to work through His Church, His Body. God does *desire* that we partner with Him so He may gain access to the earth and its systems through a people who bear His name. One purpose for congregational worship is that we aggressively affect the spirit realm with the exaltation of Jesus' name while God lets us in on the action of heavenly violence against His enemies.

So, what about those judgments of God? Since Jesus alone rules, the kingdom of God is not a democracy! As the Head of the Church, Jesus has every right to call the shots as He chooses. And we as His Body have the privilege of obeying the Ruler of all things. By virtue of our relationship to Him through His blood, we are authorized to carry out His judgments upon principalities, powers and spiritual rulers of wickedness in high places.

The Power of Truth

To practically apprehend this concept, we must continually remind ourselves that we don't fight against flesh and blood. The weapons we use are not of this natural world, but are powerfully supernatural to the point of demolishing strongholds of darkness and demonically inspired ideologies of men (see 2 Cor. 10:4). The armor of God has been explained to us throughout the years as being both defensive and offensive in function. So, looking at our primary weapon, the Sword of the Spirit, let us consider some not-so-conventional strategic uses.

We must get back to a simple understanding that nothing is more threatening to the powers of darkness than a group of believers who know their God, and who declare the Lordship of Jesus over their personal situations, their cities and their communities.

First, demonic forces in specific realms or arenas are best defeated by consistent declarations of the truth rather than by defiant personal addresses. In essence, declaring truth is the fundamental function of the Sword of the Spirit. God's Word is ultimate truth and must be proclaimed. If indeed the Church is God's voice upon the earth to communicate truth, we must develop our ability to declare and demonstrate that truth.

The most powerful truth of all time, which the Church is honored to declare, is that Jesus Christ is Lord! Nothing is more timeless in prophetic significance than that. Unfortunately, the Church in its present state has virtually underestimated the power of this truth. We've gravitated toward more sensational things to feel effective in the spirit world, often missing the most basic of all spiritual points. We must get back to a simple understanding that nothing is more threatening to the powers of darkness than a group of believers who *know* their God, and who declare the Lordship of Jesus over their personal situations, their cities and their communities.

Jesus Is Lord

Contemporarily speaking, the term "Jesus is Lord" began to be used as a catchphrase by Christians during the Jesus Movement of the late '60s. It has continued to a degree as one of those "Christianese" sayings that, sadly in many circles, has all but lost its *umph*. I remember singing the old chorus, "He is Lord, He is Lord. He is risen from the dead and He is Lord." Twenty-five years ago, that chorus was a powerful acclamation of the contemporary Church as believers from every denomination joined hands and declared together their faith in one Lord.

Today, however, it seems we've lost the simplicity of that phrase and have diminished its significance to an afterthought or a "filler phrase" with little credence. As anemic and trite as it may seem to say or sing, "Jesus is Lord," this declaration is still one of the most powerful weapons of the Church against the forces of the enemy when backed with conviction and Holy Ghost fervor. When the Spirit energizes our confessions of faith in Christ, their relevance must rise in a contemporary cultural expression. We must make them pertinent to our lives today.

God Is Looking for a Prophetic People

A quick look at biblical history beginning with Adam and proceeding to Noah, Abraham, Moses, David and Jesus, provides evidence that God has always desired a prophetic people. There is a story in Numbers 11 about Moses and 70 appointed elders who were instructed by God to assemble outside the camp in the Tent of Meeting. When the Spirit of the Lord descended upon them, they all prophesied. There was, however, a slight problem. Two of the elders didn't quite make it to the Tent in time for God's show. When the Spirit descended they began prophesying inside the camp which caused a disturbance with Joshua.

After consulting Moses, Joshua was convinced that Moses should restrain them. Moses then informed Joshua that there was no need to be jealous for his sake: "Would that all the Lord's people were prophets, that the Lord would put His Spirit upon them!" (Num. 11:29). From the mouth of one of God's prophets comes an incredible truth: God is interested in making *all* His people prophets in a very real and practical way!

Throughout the Scriptures the Lord has consistently searched for a living organism to use to demonstrate His "Godness" upon the earth. When He spoke the Word, worlds came into existence. The power of His creative Word (Jesus Christ) is the same today as He continues to locate people who will speak it and truly believe it. Thus the power of the Word is not just in the *speaking* but in the *living*.

An example of this fact is found in Noah's life. As a prophet, Noah pronounced judgment on his generation simply by building the ark (see Heb. 11:7). His obedience to God's directive became the very essence of judgment on the ancient world.

One acclamation of the Early Church was "Maranatha" (1 Cor. 16:22). To these believers "Maranatha" meant much more than "The Lord is coming." A paraphrase of this phrase could be, "The Lord comes swiftly to judge His enemies!" With a greeting and salutation such as that to open and close each worship gathering, a person would quickly develop a particular view of God as One who does not turn a blind eye or a deaf ear to the exploitation of the oppressed. As a result, "'Vengeance is mine, I will repay,' says the Lord" (see Rom. 12:19; Heb. 10:30) took on a uniquely different flavor. The retribution of God was recognized as inevitable and they participated in its preparation with the term "Maranatha!"

In Revelation 19, when John experiences the tumultuous sounds of praise and applause of God's judgment on the great harlot, he falls at the feet of one of the saints to worship. Whoever this person was, he instructs John not to do so but to "worship God. For the testimony of Jesus is the spirit of prophecy" (Rev. 19:10). What a strange statement to make after such an event! What is the point?

Though the precise interpretation of this instructional

phrase may be obscure, one thing is certain: There is a direct association with the worship of God, the testimony of Jesus and the spirit of prophecy.

Two different testimonies are mentioned in Revelation. One is the *overcomers' song* of Revelation 12:11: "And they overcame him because of the blood of the Lamb and because of the word of their testimony, and they did not love their life even unto death." The overcomers' testimony belongs to the individual who has received God's deliverance and serves as an eternal memorial before heaven's throne of God's faithfulness.

Now, let's explore the *testimony of Jesus* as it carries a much greater universal weight of prophetic significance...

To give testimony is to declare or affirm a factual truth. Borrowing from the work of the Early Church fathers, the following is a paraphrased creed filled with fundamental truths that give testimony to the eternal life of Christ and His rule:

> Jesus Christ is the only begotten, not created, Son of God,
> existent in heaven with the Father before the world began.
> He was born of the virgin Mary,
> lived a sinless life,
> began His public ministry at the age of 30,
> performed signs, wonders and miracles,
> suffered under Pontius Pilate,
> was crucified upon a cross between two thieves;
> died and was buried.
> On the third day He rose from the dead!
> Forty days later He ascended into heaven where He
> now sits at the right hand of the Father where He
> makes intercession for us.
> One day He will return to earth with His saints.
> Now He rules from the throne of heaven until His ene-
> mies are made a footstool for His feet.

These cardinal truths concerning Jesus, the Christ, are the heartbeat of prophetic utterance as they are eternal in nature and inspired by the Holy Spirit. The testimony (the record and report of witnessed evidence) of Jesus is the Spirit (breath, life, heart and essence) of prophecy (Spirit-inspired predictions and declarations of truth which lay hearts bare before God).

Jesus, having existed with God before the foundation of the world, is the beginning and end of God's message to humanity. Not only that, but when we recount His testimony in our worship, we currently witness and foretell the future demise of every opposing force to the kingdom of God!

The Hebrew word for prophesy is *naba*,[4] which means to speak under inspiration in prediction or simple discourse. Discourse, by definition, is a communication of ideas or information by way of conversation, to include speech, song or writing. Sometimes when we discuss the things of God, we are exchanging prophetic ideas through conversation and don't even know it. As His prophetic people, we have the tools to communicate God's thoughts regularly.

Employing the Hebrew word *naba*, or the Greek word *propheteia*[5] as it is used in this passage of Revelation, Spirit-inspired declarations about the life, death, resurrection and rule of Jesus are prophetic because they are *the heart of the Word of God*. In other words, Jesus is the *logos* of God or God's eternal Word. When we exalt His name, His complete work on the Cross and His righteous reign, we are prophesying or declaring God's Word in the person of Christ.

Receiving spontaneous prophetic words from the Lord in our worship services can alter our spiritual reality forever. Greater yet, however, is the kind of consistent, prophetic worship and action where the inspiration of the Holy Spirit is allowed to flow through a corporate body of people in making declarations of truth about our God—either in a predictive form, or in a forth-telling, conversational way. The consistency of this kind of worship can bring greater results in the advancement of God's kingdom when the truth is proclaimed by believing witnesses.

The plan of God for His people is prophetic in nature and has everything to do with the power of His words. Not only does He want to speak *to* His people, He desires to speak *through* His people to the inhabitants of the earth and to the powers of darkness in the heavenlies! Our corporate gatherings are much more than individuals coming together to joyously sing songs, fervently pray and recite some form of liturgy. We literally become the Body of Christ in function to facilitate the work of the Spirit as we declare eternal truths about the lordship, authority and dominion of Jesus.

The Church is God's vehicle to infiltrate the earth with His truth, so there must be a plan to spiritually do so on a regular basis rather than just by random attacks of hyped-energy blasts into the heavenlies. If we who believe don't prophetically and consistently declare His Lordship, who will?

It is crucial for us to embody now what we believe about the future. The fact that Jesus reigns through His people today is something that can be celebrated. For us, the concept of "Maranatha" is not just a subjective ideology based on centuries of speculation about God's intentions...but it is an objective reality as we see God judging His enemies in our day. The Church has the awesome responsibility to agree with heaven as it pertains to God's plan for the earth, including world evangelization and joint-heir ruling with Christ. We must learn to rejoice in God's righteous verdicts that echo heaven's rejoicing. We must allow heaven and earth to come together through us!

As God's prophetic people who are familiar with His Word, we foretell the future according to the Scriptures and forth-tell His forever current words in the life of Christ. So let us declare with confidence through our worship that:

- Jesus *is* truly Lord and reigns over all the earth from the right hand of God, regardless of what we see with our natural eyes.
- The complete redemptive work of the Cross *is* enough to save every person from hell.
- The same God who raised Jesus from the dead *is* the One who rules over the destinies of men and nations,

regardless of the seeming hopelessness of human tyranny.

- The Holy Spirit *is* definitely at work in the earth, moving men to faith and obedience, leading them to find God's will in His Word, regardless of the floundering that many experience in life.
- We are the Church of the living God who believe in Jesus as the Son of God, proclaiming forgiveness of sin and reconciliation to God, regardless of the opposition to our commission by the spirit of this age.

Throughout the past 20 or so years we've seen the abuses of inappropriate *confession*. Many have "confessed" the Word of God and used it for personal gain over and above God's purpose. Be that as it may, let us consider the truth of holy and Spirit-led confessions that are based on God's infinite wisdom and knowledge of our lives.

My pastor, Dutch Sheets, very explicitly defined biblical confession as "saying what God says." The Greek word for confession is *homologia*,[6] or "same word." Because Jesus is the High Priest of our confession (see Heb. 3:1), He can make perfect intercession for me before the Father when I agree with what He says about me and my circumstances. So, when I come to Him personally, after I empty my soul of the fear, pain or shame of life's current situations, I must say the same thing that heaven says in order to receive His fullness of grace.

With regard to corporate prophetic worship, I must say what heaven says about Jesus, the power of His blood and the authority of His kingdom. If what I see with my eyes dictates an inability to pursue faith-filled confessions, His kingdom cannot come easily, nor can His will be done in or through me.

In this prophetic sense, we are declaring God's current truth, timeless in its existence and supreme in its authority. This has the power to dismantle the kingdoms of this world and dethrone the rulers of wickedness in high places. Even now, the manifold wisdom of God is being proclaimed throughout the earth by those who believe their praises make a difference. "The wisdom which none of the rulers of this age has understood; for if they had understood it, they would not have crucified the Lord of glory" (1 Cor. 2:8)!

Why? Because now the multiplication factor has exceeded Satan's imagination. He had no clue that the Resurrection would cause his plans to blow up in his face. Had he and his minions grasped this as a possibility, they would have aborted their plans to kill Jesus in the first place. Throughout the centuries an extraordinary exponential number of believers have been "prophesying" God's current Word in the worship of Jesus Christ which has and still is displacing forces of evil in the spiritual realm!

Paul writes, "Oh, the depth of the riches both of the wisdom and knowledge of God! How unsearchable are His judgments and unfathomable His ways!" (Rom. 11:33). What an incredibly strategic and well-thought-out plan of God to utilize the praises of His people to wreak havoc with darkness.

But we must remember that we are not necessarily "special agents" for the task. Nor are we alone as we wage war on the kingdoms of darkness. There is an eternal realm that urges us onward and upward to the goals of God in this life as our prophetic praises on the earth contribute to the ultimate work of the Spirit in each generation.

The big picture includes both the realms of heaven and earth working together in cosmic chorus for the fulfillment of heaven's harmony. Our worship here is but a reflection of what is transpiring around the throne of God as the saints of all ages give glory to the Lamb in concert with the saints on the earth. One day, we will in reality join with our sainted predecessors in the eternal song that magnifies Jesus outside of time and history as the Word who holds all things together.

Notes

1. James Strong, *Strong's Exhaustive Concordance* (Nashville, Tenn.: Crusade Bible Publishers, Inc., 1983), #8416.
2. Ibid, #8605.
3. David K. Blomgren, *Restoring Praise and Worship to the Church* (Shippensburg, Pa.: Revival Press, 1989), p. 76.
4. James Strong, #5012.
5. Ibid, #4394.
6. Ibid, #3671.

JOINING HEAVEN AND EARTH

For all the saints who from their labors rest,
Who Thee by faith before the world confessed,
Thy name, O Jesus, be forever blest:
Alleluia! Alleluia!

"FOR ALL THE SAINTS"
BY WILLIAM W. HOW AND RALPH VAUGHN WILLIAMS

Have you ever wondered what the language of heaven is or what the song of heaven sounds like? What will our glorified bodies look like? Have you thought about the "Who's Who" of heaven? How about meeting the "somebodies" of the Bible? Some say there's a video room in heaven where we'll be able to see exactly how all those great biblical events took place. If this is true, I'll be first in line to see Moses part the Red Sea, David nail Goliath and Joshua raze Jericho!

The Realm Beyond

It's natural to wonder what the eternal realm will hold for us because, as regenerated beings, we will one day partake of that heavenly nature completely and in reality. As believers in Jesus Christ, our participation in the party of heaven is assured if we endure (see Col. 1:23).

The activity of the realm beyond is a fascinating concept. For centuries, people of all races and nationalities have fixated on it. Religions of every culture have tried to prepare their people for the next step in the circle of life. Those who believe in reincarnation convince themselves that death is no problem because they get to come back as a higher life-form if they've "been good" in their current one. I've often wondered what their next life experience would be if they messed up in this one!

Ancient Egyptians had an interesting view, thinking they could "take it with them" when they died. Royalty would hoard earthly treasures and servants to ensure themselves of a pleasant and prosperous afterlife. A somewhat embarrassing grimace shows up on the pages of history books, informing us of robbed graves and multimillion-dollar looting. A few centuries later, all of the precious artifacts that didn't quite make it to the final resting place of afterlife bliss disappeared. What a sad commentary on the plight of misinformed, unregenerate man. For the most part, the world's view is to seize the opportunity to get all they can and can all they get.

I am reminded of the fictitious story about a rich man who converted all his assets into gold bars before he died. Upon arriving at the gates of heaven, the man requested permission to enter with his bag of gold. Jesus approached the man to inspect the contents of his bag, and with a quizzical look responded, "Pavement?"

What we hold dear and consider precious in this life is a far cry from the glories of heaven's wonder. A brief look at the Bible's description of inside *the Gates* is proof enough that there's no comparison to the corruption of this realm. For those of us who have parents, relatives, friends and other loved ones waiting in heaven, our eyes are often fixed with anticipation upon the imminent world that is to come. For those who are not afraid of death, an internally comfortable, welcome feeling accompanies the concept of falling asleep *here* and waking up *there*.

God Needs You Here, Now!

Lest we swiftly become disheartened with our mundane lives and virtually nauseated with our present limitations, let us consider some things that can give us a vision into eternity now. Because God lives outside of time and space, *worship* of the eternal God joins us with eternity whenever we enter His presence. As a matter of fact, the moment we say yes to Jesus, our eternal destinies begin.

Jim Hodges, an instructor, mentor and spiritual father in the Lord, made the eternal realm very understandable to us as Bible School students. When people would raise questions about the coming of the Lord and how things will be once we get to heaven, he would respond, "God doesn't *need* you in heaven right now, He *needs* you on the earth. If He *needed* you in heaven, He could have arranged for you to drown in the baptistry!"

I appreciated the humor he used to communicate an extraordinary spiritual truth: There is work to be done on the earth by a covenant community of believers. By virtue of their relationship to God and fellow believers, they have accepted the challenge to live out spiritual principles on the earth and to declare regularly, "Thy kingdom come. Thy will be done, On earth as it is in heaven" (Matt. 6:10). As we discussed in the last chapter, if we don't declare God's truth upon the earth, who will?

Worship: Joining Heaven and Earth

If you've ever had the opportunity to visit or see pictures of some of the artwork in the early sixteenth-century Sistine Chapel in Rome, certainly you've noticed the great detail of Michelangelo's hand. On the vault of the papal chapel he constructed a detailed system of decoration that portrays nine scenes from the book of Genesis. These scenes include the famous "Creation of Adam" in which the fingertips of God and Adam meet. These frescoes are centrally located and surrounded by Old Testament prophets and the ancestors of Christ. Michelangelo's ceiling masterpiece in which he captured the joining of heaven and earth was a monumental task and took years to complete. It's also a beautiful representation of an eternal purpose of worship that contributes to the combined natural and supernatural sense of community.

If indeed Jesus came in the flesh to bring heaven to us instead of us to heaven, how can that happen on a practical level while we still look for that "blessed hope, the glorious appearing of our Lord and Savior" (see Titus 2:13)? One way in which the eternal purposes of heaven and earth can merge is through spirit and truth worship! When you've glimpsed heaven's wonder in worship, an awareness of unity comes with the spirit realm where time stands still and life as we know it becomes secondary to the heartbeat of God's existence.

Heaven Provides the Model for Worship

Heaven existed before earth; therefore, the model of heaven's worship supersedes that of earth. Heaven provides a perfectly complete prototype of genuine worship (see Heb. 8:5; 9:23; 12:22). The throne of heaven is God's "chair." It is not the place where He rests or relaxes—that would be the mercy seat where the blood of Jesus satisfies God's righteous and holy requirement for sin. His throne, however, is the place and position from which He rules heaven, earth and the consummate universe.

As God has received the blood of Jesus upon the mercy seat, He now rests from His labor in creation and redemption with this reward. Many sons and daughters have been brought to glory via this sacrifice (see Heb. 2:10). The true owner of the cosmos has been reinstated to righteous rule by a wooden Cross. Suspended between heaven and earth, Jesus said, "It is finished!" (John 19:30). For all practical purposes, Jesus may as well have said, "The purchase is complete. I now present the earth and its fullness back to You, Father!" The most incredible event in history has been recorded in the annals of heaven, bringing the worship of the Creator into another dimension with a new title, "Redeemer."

Now sitting on the throne, He exercises His governmental role as Ruler of all. Jesus is the focus and "object" of our worship, as He is the One who made it possible for us to minister before the throne of God.

Heaven's Worship Is Eternal

Though our ministry before the throne will be without end, the concept of eternity mystifies us. To think that the worship of God will go on for eternity is mind-boggling. We sometimes wonder, *Won't we get tired? Won't we run out of things to say*

Worship is one occupation that will last forever!

and sing? I once heard someone describe the cherubim and seraphim in heaven: They cover their eyes with their wings. When they uncover them and look upon the Lamb, they see a brand-new facet of His glorious being, to which they respond with a freshly invigorated and thunderous, "Holy, holy, holy!"— and this goes on forever!...and ever...(compare with Rev. 4:8)!

The eternal nature of worship is what makes this aspect of the Church's ministry so important. Worship is one occupation that will last forever! However valid many Christian activities are, they are but a temporary overflow of the life we have in Jesus that is meant to be shared with others. As an instructor of missiology and a strong advocate of the Great Commission, John Piper writes,

> Missions is not the ultimate goal of the church. Worship is. Missions exists because worship doesn't. Worship is ultimate, not missions, because God is ultimate, not man. When this age is over, and the countless millions of the redeemed fall on their faces before the throne of God, missions will be no more. It is a temporary necessity. But worship abides forever.[1]

The focus on worship as the priority is an incredibly powerful concept that is often overlooked in the Church. *We see worship as a means to an end rather than the focus of our being.* We sometimes feel a need to "get on with Kingdom business" after we've worshiped as if it were a warm-up to greater challenges ahead of us. What's wrong with this idea? Sure we are to "act" out our faith and "demonstrate" that we are putting feet to our prayers. After all, "faith without works is useless" (Jas. 2:20). However, if Jesus is the Alpha and Omega (see Rev. 1:8; 22:13) and our worship of Him is the beginning and the end, then everything in between must be related somehow to worship.

The Eternal Body of Christ

In the realm of the eternal, those who have gone to be with Christ in heaven can somehow coach us in our walk of faith. "Therefore, since we have so great a cloud of witnesses surrounding us, let us also lay aside every encumbrance, and the sin which so easily entangles us, and let us run with endurance the race that is set before us" (Heb. 12:1). This verse says they are surrounding us. This is the basis for the statement in the early creeds, "I believe...in the communion of saints." That would mean they have some knowledge of our progress in the things of the Spirit. Though we cannot see them, we can take comfort in the presence of those who have "been there and done that" and are alive today to encourage us from another dimension!

Williams's translation says, "There's a vast crowd of spectators in the grandstands." The same witnesses encouraging us in life's race are the witnesses who behold the face of God as they sing songs of His greatness and worth. Perhaps they look over the portals of heaven as we worship on the earth and say, "Yes! Keep up the good work for the Kingdom! Enter into this dimension a little further; we know there's something special from His heart waiting for you!" Knowing that we are joined by countless millions of others who have partaken in the struggle of faith and have now risen to the joy of the final overcoming can give us a great sense of completion.

When we share a difficult experience with another person, a common bond of understanding permeates that relationship. When we endure hardship for the sake of the Cross, we can draw strength from knowing that we are in good company with men and women of faith. Through our worship we can join with those who can relate to the emotional and physical sufferings we experience—those who have been faithful through the ages in their walk with God.

Heaven's Worship Themes

The themes of heaven's worship have substantial value for us today as they are eternal and we will be singing them for ages to come. Let's look into John's revelation to see who is saying what.

Holy

The creatures are ever crying "Holy," acknowledging God as the only unique Supreme Being "who was and is and is to come."

And the four living creatures, each one of them having six wings, are full of eyes around and within; and day and night they do not cease to say, "Holy, Holy, Holy, is the Lord God, the Almighty, who was and who is and who is to come" (Rev. 4:8).

When we echo heaven's declarations of "Holy, holy, holy" in our earthly worship, we invite the transforming presence of God's holiness to change us. It's one thing to sing about God's attributes, but it's entirely different to be transformed by the revelation of experiencing one of those attributes.

I remember a worship service where we were singing about the holiness of God. There was an awesome awareness of His presence as we sang. Suddenly, the room was filled with a charge of energy that swept us into a loud shout of "HOLY!" Together we saw Him in His holy light and were compelled to voice what we saw. It seemed almost irreverent to "shout" HOLY, primarily because we'd always expressed holy in hushed adoration. But in that moment, we had to join heaven's living creatures in loud acclamation to practice for the eternal.

Worthy

The 24 elders are cited in two places to be lifting songs to the worth of the Lamb. First, they sang:

Worthy art Thou, our Lord and our God, to receive glory and honor and power; for Thou didst create all things, and because of Thy will they existed, and were created (Rev. 4:11).

Because of His blood poured out for the sins of the world, Jesus is worthy to receive the highest praise, honor and recognition. Until we identify with His sacrifice, we cannot fully appreciate what He did. His blood was the payment required to purchase our souls from the dregs of darkness. Only when we see how far we've fallen from the mercy of God can we stand in a humbly confident place of worship, saying, "You are worthy, Lamb of God."

In the glory of His loving redemption, nothing compares with the power of His blood to cleanse. Years ago when I was grappling with the Cross, the Lord needed to bring me down to the basics of my existence to prove that what I had to offer Him was worthless apart from what He had to offer me. In my state of total worthlessness, He showed me what He was worth and chose to "change clothes" with me. He exchanged His robe of priceless beauty for my filthy rags of self-righteousness and died with my clothes on. What else can be said here but a humble, "Thank You, Jesus!" with a heart that is bowed down in gratitude and worship to Him.

The second song the 24 elders sang was:

Worthy art Thou to take the book, and to break its seals; for Thou wast slain, and didst purchase for God with Thy blood men from every tribe and tongue and people and nation. And Thou hast made them to be a kingdom and priests to our God; and they will reign upon the earth (Rev. 5:9,10).

Jesus is worthy to receive glory because He created all things. And He's worthy to open the scroll because He redeemed all things. Have you ever wondered what the scroll is? Mike Bickle shares the following powerful personal insight:

To open the scroll, one takes responsibility for its contents. The sacred scroll is God's plan of redemption, the title deed to the earth, the plan of God for ages past in the hands of Jesus. It is the only thing that touches the throne of God, and Jesus is in the center of that throne.[2]

The exercise of Jesus' power and authority in opening the holy scroll proves His worth through His ownership of the planet. The act of creation and the act of redemption display not only His rights to the earth but also His heart for its inhabitants. For the Creator Himself to die for His creation in order to purchase those He created is nothing short of awe-some love—not to mention the legal ramifications of His blood payment.

The Song of Moses and the Lamb

This is a prophetic song of deliverance as sung by those who overcame the beast:

> Great and marvelous are Thy works, O Lord God, the Almighty; Righteous and true are Thy ways, Thou King of the nations. Who will not fear, O Lord, and glorify Thy name? For Thou alone art holy; for all the nations will come and worship before Thee, for Thy righteous acts have been revealed (Rev. 15:3,4).

I've always been fascinated at the categorization of this song to include Moses and Jesus in tandem. Both were the Bible's greatest deliverers *and* intercessors. So, what of the prophetic significance of paralleled covenants in this deliverer's duet? Is it possible that the joining of the covenants through this song announced the end of the first covenantal age? Perhaps the voicing of this prophetic melody in the corridors of heaven's glory resounded to the ages past, present and future that the "new age" had begun—the age of Christ's rule over every kind of bondage imaginable.

Here, the multitudes in heaven are worshiping, "Great and marvelous are Your deeds." They are recognizing God's creation and His redemption. Both are acts of power where life springs forth from nonlife or death.

Hallelujah

Have you ever sung a sweet song of hallelujah? Sometimes we spontaneously sing a rendition of "Alleluia" that is very wor-shipful and "holy" sounding. Some may feel that they've reached a level of sacred, euphoric bliss when they finally arrive at the harmonic "hallelujah" point. There's nothing wrong with this kind of quiet and sensitive worship. However, the precedent set in heaven is much more robust than our sometimes sweet and anemic, yet sincere, hallelujah offerings in worship.

The Scripture shows that the saints in heaven join their voices with the entire heavenly host and the sound is like the roar of many waters and peals of thunder as they *shout*,

"Hallelujah! Salvation and glory and power belong to our God; because His judgments are true and righteous...." And again, "Hallelujah! For the Lord our God, the Almighty, reigns" (Rev. 19:1,6).

Their shouts of "hallelujah" ring out through the halls of heaven and the corridors of time to declare awesome truths. The judgments of God are righteous and true for HE REIGNS!

It would not be wise to dismiss the intensity with which these truths are declared, as God's judgments have eternal value and are outside of time and space. He is decreeing them as you read. Our response to His judgments released on the earth can be, "Oh God, must You do that?" OR, "Hallelujah, Your work is perfect and all Your ways are just! Do as You will and let Your glory be made known to the ends of the earth!"

You've probably heard the phrase, "being on the same page." Singing "holy," "worthy" and "hallelujah" puts us on the same page as heaven's choirs. For our present-day cybersociety, it could be called heaven's "web" page. If all we ever did was sing "hallelujah" to the worth of the Holy Lamb of God, we would be current with the eternal macro chemistry of ancient glory; for He was, and is, and is to come!

Shouts Are Often Birthed Out of Silence

Though much of what we are discussing in this chapter has to do with vocalizing our praise, I want to make it clear that silence also has its place in worship. Often before we can come to the throne to worship, we must spend contemplative time in prayer, meditation and listening to God's voice. We must not forget, "Be still, and know that I am God" (Ps. 46:10, *NIV*).

This idea of being still is spoken to the troubled soul and is in the context of worrying about life's situations. The quiet place of personal pursuit is usually necessary to bring us to the realization that all that we need, He is for us. Thus He assures us in Isaiah 30:15 that "In repentance and rest you shall be saved, in quietness and trust is your strength." Quiet times are needed to maintain a holy walk.

The Highway of Worship

God has designed a path for us to travel on. It's called "the Highway of Holiness" (Isa. 35:8). Jesus called the gate to life small and the way narrow and added that only a few would find it (see Matt. 7:14).

Though not wide, by any stretch of the imagination, many can travel on the Highway of Holiness together because Jesus bought our traveling privileges with His priceless blood. His plan is for all to come to repentance and a knowledge of God. So perhaps we could paraphrase His words: "Crimson is the way, beginning at Calvary's cross, that leads to the presence of the Father. Many will be offended at My suffering which paves the way and will not choose this path."

The words of the prophet Isaiah clearly point to some sort of offense in the way: "Make smooth in the desert a highway for our God" (Isa. 40:3). Also, "Clear the way for the people; build up, build up the highway" (Isa. 62:10). As the Scriptures unfold we see the offense in the road is the Messiah Himself (see Ps. 118:22; Isa. 8:14; Rom. 9:33; 1 Pet. 2:8). The ancient Yahweh is revealed through the Messiah as Abba Father and the way to get to Him is through the suffering death of His Son. To those who thought Messiah would usher in a physical kingdom of God, it's no wonder they were completely offended at God's methodology.

Psalm 68:4 indicates that the Highway sometimes winds through the wilderness. As we walk through times of barrenness, worship creates an avenue for the Lord's refreshing.

Most scholars believe that Psalms 120—134, known as the "Song of Degrees or Song of Ascents," were sung or recited while traveling up the hill to Jerusalem during times of pilgrimage for the feasts. Could it be possible that as we worship the Father we are gradually becoming more like Jesus by partaking of His divine nature on the Highway of Holiness? Second Peter 1:3,4 says that His divine power has given us everything we need for life and godliness through our knowledge of Him. These great and precious promises are provided so we might become partakers of the divine nature and escape the corruption of the world.

To take communion is to partake of the divine nature...and to accept His invitation to a precious and holy meal that can only be enjoyed as we place our affections on Him through worship.

Laying hold of the great and precious promises can sometimes slip through our grasp and "holding on for dear life," as it has been stated, is not too far from the truth on occasion. It's an all too familiar feeling to slide off the Highway of Holiness when we lose our grip on the promises of God. At that point, we need a spiritual rescue operation to get us back on track. We must re-confess that He's given us everything necessary for life and godliness in our knowledge of Him. It can simply be in the form of some personal pep talk that gets us over the hump, back on the road and ready to sit at His table again.

To take communion is to partake of the divine nature (see 2 Pet. 1:4) and to accept His invitation to a precious and holy meal that can only be enjoyed as we place our affections on Him through worship. This is where you and I find that we can do nothing outside of His grace and mercy. In other words, I need Him to once again assume the role of Master and Savior to deliver me from myself. The art of abiding is a cultivated process whereby He imparts His life as I give up mine. I do this by continually acknowledging Him as Lord of my deepest parts. An impartation of His holiness is what follows, where I am embraced in the heart-to-heart communion that I so long for.

From Sinai to Mount Zion

This highway of holiness, paved by the King Himself, leads us "to Mount Zion and to the city of the living God, the heavenly Jerusalem, and to myriads of angels, to the general assembly and church of the first-born who are enrolled in heaven, and to God, the Judge of all, and to the spirits of righteous men made perfect, and to Jesus, the mediator of a new covenant, and to the sprinkled blood, which speaks better than the blood of Abel" (Heb. 12:22-24).

The writer of Hebrews is making a contrast of worship experiences between that of Old Covenant Sinai (Heb. 12:18-21) and New Covenant Zion (Heb. 12:22-24). God visited Moses on Mount Sinai in the wilderness but the psalmist said God lived on Mount Zion. Thus God wants to takes us from "Sinai" to "Zion" as we travel the Highway of Holiness.

The Highway is a two-way street. Not only do we move toward Him on this path but the Lord also travels toward us upon it to escort us to the place of rest where we can abide with Him in His holy habitation.

Saint Augustine once prayed, "O God, Thou hast made us for Thyself and our souls are restless, searching until they find their rest in Thee."[3] How true this is! So often we strive and labor to enter His rest (see Heb. 4:11), that when we finally get there, we don't know what to do. To experientially arrive at Mount Zion in a worship gathering is unfortunately a rarity. Jesus told those who were weary and burdened to come to Him for rest. When we ultimately acknowledge that He is speaking to us, we sometimes feel let down and defeated, being forced to admit our inability to keep up the high-energy charade for the sake of the Kingdom's progress. The alternative to the internal rest of Mount Zion is the external performance necessary to make Mount Sinai livable. Is there really a choice to be considered?

The Highway of Holiness has been traveled over the years by the saints who have gone before. God paved it with the blood of His Son and His saints may travel it freely because He paid the price. However, religious counterfeits stand at its entrance, demanding that the road be repaved with human effort and sacrifice. Religion, however, is merely humanity's attempts to please God, nullifying the work of grace we experience through His free, sacrificial gift paid for on the Cross. Therefore, to ascend the Highway with fleshly efforts in an attempt to please God is impossible!

God has designed the Highway of Holiness to bring us near to Himself. Jude 14 says Enoch prophesied that He saw the Lord descending with many thousands of His saints. I like to think that when we worship, the Lord meets us on the Highway with those thousands of saints (also known as the great cloud of witnesses) and escorts us into the glorious arena of the eternal.

We worship to attain a greater awareness of who God is and who He's called us to be as His people. We do this by entering into all that He has provided for us.

God did not stop creating on the sixth day. He merely called us into a place of rest where we could discover even more about His creativity. He is the epitome of creativity and He's still in the business of creating today through His people. The sanctified imagination of a redeemed soul is a tool in the hand of the Master Craftsman. When the creative gift is submitted to

God, He can use it to demonstrate His life through that individual and cause His message to be heard via the medium of art. Because the Spirit is at work in the earth drawing humanity to Jesus, He's looking for living vessels through whom He can pour His creativity for the purpose of glorifying the Creator and proving HE IS.

Notes

1. John Piper, *Let the Nations Be Glad* (Grand Rapids, Mich.: Baker Books, 1996), p. 11.
2. Mike Bickle, *"The Thunder of God's Passion,"* Colorado Springs, Co.: June 23, 1997.
3. T. P. Carter, *Jokes, Notes and Quotes* (Columbus, Ga.: Quill Publications, 1991), p. 66.

CREATIVE WORSHIP

Joyful, joyful, we adore Thee, God of glory, Lord of love.
Hearts unfold like flowers before Thee,
opening to the sun above.
Melt the clouds of sin and sadness, drive the
dark of doubt away;
Giver of immortal gladness, fill us with the light of day.

"JOYFUL, JOYFUL, WE ADORE THEE"
BY HENRY VAN DYKE, LUDWIG VAN BEETHOVEN
(MELODY FROM NINTH SYMPHONY)

Saint Mary's Cathedral in Bury Saint Edmonds, Suffolk, England, was full of energy as the worshipers gathered to participate in a unique service of praise. This was an historical moment. The atmosphere was charged with a sense of eager expectation as people anticipated a visitation from the Spirit of God in this 400-year-old, stoic house of worship.

The meeting began with the sound of the shofar and a procession complete with banners declaring, "The Lord Reigns," "Holy, Holy, Holy," "Blessing, Glory, Honor, Praises" and "The earth shall be filled with the knowledge of the glory of the Lord...." Dancers with tambourines and streamers began to move up the aisles as the worship team sang, "Prepare ye the way of the Lord."

An awesome explosion of praise resulted. The people rose to their feet in applause at the entrance of the Lord of glory and exuberantly rejoiced in the fresh awakening of the Spirit. The numerous saints buried under the floor must have sensed a wave of exhilaration in heaven. After all, worship is what this building was designed for!

Declaring His Majesty

That was May of 1994. I was asked to lead a team of worshipers and intercessors to England. Joining with another worship team, the plan was to visit several cathedrals in Great Britain to declare the majesty of God in ancient places of worship. While praying, the British organizers of these events sensed the focus of the meetings should display the majesty of God through visual demonstrations of worship in pageantry. These majestic times of tribute to the King of kings would be followed by a challenging word from my friend and colaborer, Dutch Sheets. So combining the British and American teams, we did just that for 10 days.

Traveling to various parts of England, we watched the Lord unfold His splendor in worship as we creatively declared His praise with visual demonstrations. The use of dance and banners provided a means of expression that few had experienced before in a worship gathering. When these believers observed the literal beauty of His presence, a new and unique dimension was added to their worship repertoire. Many began to understand the "splendor of His majesty" and the "beauty of His holiness."

I later learned that shortly after our trip, a significant visitation of the Holy Spirit came to some churches in London. What role we played as vessels of His glory, only eternity will tell.

In looking at her history, the throne of the United Kingdom has been in the spotlight as an important world "player" for more than 800 years. Though history has confirmed corruption and abuses of power and authority within the empire, spiritual significance can be linked to all the regalia, pomp and circumstance of state. The crown itself symbolizes and depicts the resplendent awe and glory of the monarchy. What was God's original intention for England? What would be His redemptive purpose for that land so rich in nobility, culture, ethics, protocol and yes, even pride? Could it be that His plan is to use the picture of England's monarchy to grant us a glimpse of His splendor and majesty? I believe it is.

Hallelujah: Praise to God!

Praise is the way we usher in His Majesty. So let's look again at the meaning of "praise." To reiterate, several Hebrew and Greek words for praise are used throughout the Scriptures, each one having specific significance when used in various contexts. One word that has seen much use in the Hebrew is *halal*. This is a unique word that has several meanings. We get the word "hallelujah" from it, which literally means "praise to Jah," or "Yah," the first syllable of the divine name "Yahweh" (see Exod. 13:14). Yet the vastness of the root meaning of this word encompasses more than just a directive to praise God.

Halal can mean "to be clear (originally of sound but usually of color); to shine; to make a show, to boast; and thus to be (clamorously) foolish; to rave; to celebrate...glory."[1]

Although we can find many examples of the word *halal* in the Bible, let's focus on Jeremiah 9:24 for now:

"But let him who boasts [*halal*] boast of this, that he understands and knows Me, that I am the Lord who exercises lovingkindness, justice, and righteousness on earth; for I delight in these things," declares the Lord.

Our celebration in the sanctuary and the *halal* we raise in our demonstrations of praise is based on our knowledge of God and His ways upon the earth. So, our boasting or celebrating is indeed a response to knowing God! The way in which each local fellowship celebrates depicts its unique distinctives in understanding God and His ways.

The Exodus Event and the Christ Event

Old Testament worship was based on an historical event known as the Exodus. The art of celebration in Israel was intrinsically linked to their deliverance from 400 years of Egyptian bondage. Throughout their history, the Jews were instructed by the prophets to remember the slavery of old and to give thanks to the God of their fathers.

> *If we want His resurrection life to infuse our mortal bodies, we must make it clear that we believe it's possible to benefit now from something that happened so long ago!*

New Testament worship is based on an historical event we know as "The Christ Event," including His resurrection and ascension. Worship renewal pioneer Robert Webber says, "Worship tells and acts out the life, death, resurrection, and coming again of Christ through the proclamation of the Word and the Table."[2]

As we gather to worship on Sundays, we celebrate the resurrection of Jesus on the first day of the week; we also reexperience the joy and reality of this 2,000-year-old event! The Resurrection is a prophetically current event that when celebrated, releases both the historical and spiritual blessings inherent in its genetic chromosomal makeup.

The fact that we celebrate Jesus' life today is a worthy investment of time and energy. If we want His resurrection life to infuse our mortal bodies, we must make it clear that we believe it's possible to benefit now from something that happened so long ago!

This momentous occurrence has the right to take center stage in the theater of eternity while all of humankind marvels in awe at the way Jesus righteously defeated the devil. Our Sunday worship celebrations should cause the world's concept of "PARTY" to pale by comparison. We should spare nothing in our expense for the expressions of joy in the life that has been purchased for us!

Ancient civilizations were built around the worship of their gods. The Hebrews began their worship culture by centering it around the wilderness Tabernacle which housed the presence of God. God was central and the worship of His name was the highest priority in all of society. Even the gifts and trades of both men and women contributed to the furnishings of the Tent of Worship. The people felt honored to beautify God's praise with their crafts.

Psalm 66:1,2 says, "Shout joyfully to God. Sing the glory of His name; make His praise *glorious*" (italics added). In other words, see to it that the praise of His name is made beautiful. This is not a "closed eye" operation. We're talking about the visual impact of worship expressions giving way to more understanding and appreciation of God's creativity!

Make His Praise Glorious

To "make His praise glorious" is to create ways in which He can be honored by the investment He's made in us. Think of the gifts and talents He's placed in us that lie buried beneath the surface of bondage we commonly place on ourselves. We erroneously think, *God wouldn't be interested in using* that *part of my life's experience.* Perhaps people have told us there's no room in the Kingdom for something as carnal as...let's say, woodwork or art or dance, for example. So we've done the spiritually "noble" thing and left that talent outside the confines of our worship. God's investment of creativity is now being treated as refuse and rubbish because we've missed His intention to redeem all things for His glory.

The redemptive heart of God is always on display in the face of Jesus. Things we think are of no value or consequence, He shines His resurrection light on and brings back to life. The reason? To prove that He is the Resurrection and the Life and worthy to be celebrated in the most demonstrative and obvious ways! So we boast in Him, we glory, we shine, we rave, we dance, we sing and allow the use of colorful visuals in worship to become a literal function of the word *halal*.

Show Forth His Praise

As we make His praise glorious, we also show forth His praise. In the apostle Peter's first letter to the churches of Asia Minor he writes, "But you are A CHOSEN RACE...that you may proclaim [*show forth*] the excellencies of Him who has called you out of darkness into His marvelous light" (1 Pet. 2:9, italics added).

This term "show forth" (Greek: *exagello*)[3] means "to publish, celebrate, to demonstrate." The instruction given here is to demonstrate the praise of the One who called us out of darkness. We are to publicly announce, celebrate and demonstrate our deliverance from the kingdom of darkness.

Our demonstration of personal and corporate testimony, as we've already discussed, takes many different forms of biblical expression such as singing, shouting, lifting our hands, clapping, playing musical instruments, standing, kneeling, bowing, prostrating our bodies before Him and dancing. The emotional impact of these expressions can be heightened by the freedom we are granted to use them or demonstrate them in a given service of worship.

When we begin to contemplate and fully appreciate the difference between the kingdoms of light and darkness, there is an ignition of something holy that must give way to expression. It is impossible to quench this expression for any length of time and still expect the fire to burn.

Dance: The Body Language of Heaven

The Gnostics of the first and second centuries believed that the spirit was imprisoned in the body, so the mind/spirit was "good" and the body was evil. The dance in Christian worship was, therefore, marked by vehement church leaders insistent on squelching it as an expression of praise.

"By 1700 religious dancing either disappeared, survived in isolated places, changed into folk or court expressions, or remained nearly indiscernible. From the period in which dance was accepted first by pagans and then by Jews and finally allowed by Christians, through the period of suspicion and then ever-increasing prohibitions, dance finally was forced out of its place in the liturgical celebrations of the church. Society first relegated dance to use in its courtly ceremonies and then developed it into the sophistication of the ballet. Dance was given back totally to society, with a few exceptions remaining of Church-related Christian dance."[4]

I believe dance is one of the many ways in which we use all of who we are to worship all of who He is.

We Worship with All of Our Being

The first commandment exhorts us to love the Lord with all of our heart, mind, soul and strength. In Old Testament language, the heart is synonymous with the depths of the soul or the subconscious mind. Sometimes the word "heart" is used to refer to the spirit of man. (Worship that is heart only is incomplete. God is looking for action to accompany heart motivation.) As most are aware, the mind is the consciousness or thought processor while the soul involves the will and the emotions.

To give God "all that is within me" is saying that my feelings, desires, ambitions, affections, motivations (understood or not), and physical strength are being released to give honor to the Creator of those things. When I give thanks to God "with all my heart," I am acknowledging that even the things I am not aware of in the depths of my subconscious mind—i.e., arguments, turmoils, unanswered questions, hidden agendas, selfish plans and the like— are laid open and bare before the light of His glorious presence. Nothing is hidden from Him...though some-times in reality it may be hidden from me.

God has created us multidimensional. We are spiritual, physiological, psychological, emotional and social creatures. To agree with the Gnostics that we are solely "mind and spirit beings" encased in a robe of evil flesh is to deny the vastness of our humanity ordained by God. He created us with all these interwoven parts to bring genuine *fullness* to our lives. Submitting all our "parts" to Him is our gift of worship.

I've encountered people who choose to downplay their humanity to such a degree that they don't allow themselves to be affected emotionally by anything unless it is under their control. Their lack of passion is often mistaken as "spirit-controlled-emotions" but actually represents "will-controlled-emotions." You've most likely heard the phrase, "Control yourself," meaning "Show some self-control" with regard to your emotions. Though the will-based aspect of self-control keeps me from doing stupid things (such as going to the grocery store naked) in order to fit into society, remember that self-control is a fruit of the Spirit. That does not mean that I must deny my emotions in order to prove my holiness. It means that I do not allow this one aspect of my being to have rule, power and authority over me.

Emotions are God's gift to us to keep us from becoming totally left-brained "Vulcans" such as Dr. Spock from *Star Trek* who showed absolutely no emotion. Bob Sorge writes, "While praise is not emotionalism, it is emotional. It is most fitting to praise the Lord in an emotional manner. God created our emo-tions, and praise is the noblest way to release our emotions."[5] Creating avenues to return our emotions to God is our gift to Him.

Considering the impact of aesthetics, beauty and art in wor-ship, Tim Keller writes, "Our mind, will and emotions are all organically connected. Art, which is ingested through the right side of the brain, is the back door to the left side or the ana-lytical part of the brain."[6]

How often do you find yourself moved with emotion at a tender moment in a movie? You may completely disagree with the character's philosophy of life or style, yet when presented with an emotional exchange about a real-life issue, you are touched. Suddenly, it matters little that you cannot analyze that person's behavior. The point is, you've connected with that character on an emotional level which supersedes philosophical rhetoric and demeanor. That character becomes human and worth the time you're investing in this experience.

Something similar transpires when we are confronted with visual beauty in worship. If we allow ourselves to see it and acknowledge it as a vehicle for understanding God on a deeper level (that is, deeper than just the conscious mind), we can often look beyond the imperfect human vessel demonstrating the act of worship and appreciate that person's heart for God.

I remember the first time I saw a performance by Ballet Magnificat. The artistic director, Kathy Thibideaux, performed a dance rendition to "We Shall Behold Him." Dressed in a long, white, flowing gown, she interpreted the vocal piece in a visual way. Something brand-new happened to that song that day. It was no longer just in my imagination or my mind's eye—I actually experienced a portion of the joy of the ultimate Christ event! Though I'd heard about this awaited event most of my life, I had never been moved in this way before. The aesthetic beauty of her craft in movement touched something deep in my soul that transcended all the teachings and preachings on the subject of the Lord's return.

The use of one's artistic craft in worship takes us to a level of truly appreciating both God's creation and His creativity as it is released through His people. The opportunity to receive God's grace through artistic means and have our lives eternally changed is a unique gift we should gratefully receive. As Robert Webber says, "Festivity puts us in touch with another realm of life—the fanciful and imaginative."[7]

One thing the Church could use a whole lot more of is true imagination and celebration (not to be confused with fantasy and frivolity). Our lives are filled with enough serious decisions to be made as responsibilities loom over us to the point of causing stress-related diseases and depression. We need time to be festive and celebrate His resurrection life in us. To show forth His praise is to clearly announce and declare His worth in celebration through vocal and visual means.

Liturgical Worship

Have you ever been to a formal, liturgical church and experienced the pageantry of worship—the color, the smell of incense, the sounds and the sense of history? For some, this kind of worship is all too familiar and something they wish to run from. But for others it's an intriguing picture of order, majesty and beauty. So what's the idea being presented here? Apparently, it's not just traditional ritualism that propels these worshipers week after week. They must have a reason other than habit for their methods of worship. In most cases, if you dig for it, you can find an element of Spirit-inspired revelation that leads to the establishment of a tradition.

For those who have been raised in this kind of atmosphere, the purpose for all the pageantry may be easy to explain. The fact remains that the formality of this flavor is appealing to many believers for scores of reasons, many of which are deeply personal. Interestingly, in the United States, many young urban professionals are investigating and returning to more liturgical churches. Perhaps this return represents reconnecting with the faith of our fathers that makes them feel "safe" in this unpredictable world.

With all the questionable flamboyance on the part of some high-profile spiritual leaders, it's no wonder the safety factor plays such a significant role in the decision-making process of these young people. The safe place is a church that's been around for a long time and intends to remain when others decide to fold.

Whether it be in an established liturgical church or in a contemporary-flavored congregation, people are usually looking for security and safety from bona fide leadership that genuinely cares about them! Thus, if God is experienced in the truth of His love, there can be an embrace of His ways regardless of the flavor of the worship.

Seeing Helps Believing

One of the ways God communicates His love is through visual art. The eye gate is a means whereby the world has monopolized the affections and desires of humanity. The lust of the eyes is one of the three things that are of the world and not of the Father, according to 1 John 2:16. As we reflect on God's purposes for His people, redemption is in His heart! He desires to reveal the genuine in order to unmask and deflate the counterfeit. If the counterfeit of God's splendor and beauty is something carnal and temporal, is there really a choice to be made?

When I see a depiction of God's spiritual and eternal reality displayed on a natural plane, God is brought to a level in my understanding where I can choose His transformation in my mind, heart AND spirit. One of the ways that God becomes real is through the visual arts.

Worship and the Visual Arts

In her book, *Celebration: Banners, Dance and Holiness in Worship*, Lora Allison beautifully articulates and practically illustrates the use of colorful celebration art in worship. The parallel between worship and warfare shows up clearly in this study of banners and flags.

Historically and biblically, the use of banners and flags dates back to more than 3000 B.C. The following provides a view of their historical as well as their contemporary usage:

1. *Banners rally the troops for war.* [In *Webster's Dictionary*] under the word "banner," the first definition is, "a piece of cloth attached by one edge to a staff and used by a monarch, feudal lord or commander as a rallying point for the troops."

2. *Banners bestow honor.* Second definition: "an ensign displaying a distinctive or symbolic device or legend; especially one presented as an award of honor or distinction."

3. *Banners tell people whom you represent.* "A name, slogan, or goal associated with a particular group or ideology."

4. *Banners signal or attract attention.* The last definition we will use comes under "flag." "Usually a rectangular piece of fabric of distinctive design that is used as a symbol or signaling device."

5. *Banners herald an event.*

6. *Banners unify the company, directing the warfare.* Egyptians flew the first flaglike symbols. Soldiers would carry poles with long streamers attached, and in the battle they would watch to see which way the wind was blowing in order to aim their arrows.

7. *Banners show victories won.* Even today it is the custom for army units to display a chronicle of victories won by streamers tied to their standards.

8. *Banners are a demonstration of God's presence in our midst.* In Exodus 17:15, when Moses erected an altar and named it "Jehovah Nissi" (the Lord our banner), he was recognizing the presence of the mighty Jehovah alive in their midst.

9. *Banners can be a rallying point of healing.* In Numbers 21 we read of the fiery serpents that came to bite and kill the people. When the people repented, the Lord instructed Moses to make a bronze serpent and set it on a standard. This rallying point of healing and life was a prophetic symbol of the Greater to come.

10. *Banners put the enemy to flight.* "So (as the result of the Messiah's intervention) they shall (reverently) fear the name of the Lord from the west, and His glory from the rising of the sun. When the enemy shall come in like a flood, the Spirit of the Lord will lift up

a standard against him and put him to flight—for He
will come like a rushing stream which the breath of
the Lord drives" (Isa. 59:19, *Amp.*).

ll. Banners minister to and celebrate the Lord. "And in the
name of our God we will set up our banners" (Ps. 20:5).[8]

If we look at the practical uses of flags and banners in history,
we see their relevance is still employed by every nation upon
the earth. Applying the already established biblical ideas of visual worship, the principles of worship and warfare are strongly
supported in the use of banners and flags that make statements
of God's character and how He should be worshiped.

Flags bring a sense of belonging. They help us remember that
we are connected. They remind us of our roots and unify us for
the future. They provide a sense of sacred identity. In America, for
example, to damage the flag can bring about legal ramifications.
We wave flags to celebrate our independence; we lower flags to
display our mourning. In some countries the flag is raised when
the leader is in the palace and lowered when the leader is out of
the country. How much more should we use flags and banners to
let the world know that we are united, we have received our independence from the works of hell and darkness, and the King of
kings is at all times seated on the throne in our behalf!

Throughout the years, many have passed swift judgment
about various forms of visual worship expression, including
flags, banners, art and dance, saying, "That's too conspicuous,"
or, "That draws too much attention to itself rather than to
God," or, "You're worshiping the expression itself." Though
room to evaluate motives always exists, a brief reminder of the
definition of *halal* includes being conspicuous; to rave or to
shine. The expressions we use in worship *are* to draw attention.
The purpose is to show that God is worth the excellence of an
extravagant display of classic and dramatic action and beauty!

We live in a day when the Body of Christ is becoming
more aware of one another. I believe we are approaching a
time when the spirit of unity will be so prevalent that we are

able to lower our boundaries to the point of genuine appreciation of our differences rather than just tolerance. Please don't confuse what I'm saying with condoning compromise or evil practices. On the contrary, with eyes wide open, we can behold the glory of God in the members of His Body in our communities and around the globe to such a degree that we are able to say with joy, "Viva la Difference!" All that God has created is GOOD!

Once when criticized for his particular methodology, Smith Wigglesworth said, "Well, I like the way I do it better than the way you don't." We must keep in mind the fact that we see through a glass dimly and that our perspectives are limited in light of the eternal. It's easy to become careless in our opinions about how we worship when we are uninformed of God's relevant dealings outside our spheres of experience, knowledge and influence.

For some, true worship will include a pipe organ introit, accompanying the clergy's processional with vestments and candles. For others it is an hour of intimate love songs to Jesus in casual attire led with a guitar (and don't forget all the forms and styles in between).

The Dramatic Arts

Because of cultural and historical precedents, we are usually comfortable with what we have been exposed to and taught to accept. However, one of the facets of worship that God is using more and more to communicate spiritual truths in a way that is palatable to virtually every culture is the dramatic arts.

"All across the globe, drama is proving to be an extremely effective tool....I believe it's because drama follows Jesus' model for effective communication. Jesus constantly used parables, stories from daily life and word pictures that grabbed His listeners' minds and hearts."[9]

Studies have shown that the left side of the brain is logical, linear, black-and-white and judgmental. The left brain asks,

What are the rules? The right side, however, houses the intuitive, artistic and emotional characteristics. The right brain asks, How does it feel? The lack of balance between the two sides of the brain can imperil our understanding.

For example, recently my son, Collin, was in trouble with his teacher at school. We found that his attention span even for a 7-year-old was extremely short. He was having terrible difficulty "listening" in class and following directions for projects. Not only was he falling behind in his school work, but he was also becoming a "pill" at home. Collin began to show signs of hyperactivity and attention deficit disorder. So our family doctor prescribed a battery of tests that put him within the margins of such a diagnosis. Our choices were slim: either endure and hope he would outgrow it, or resort to medication.

We knew there had to be another solution. Then we heard about a brain-patterning technique from a friend who put us in contact with Becky Kennard, author and developer of a brain integration program known as "Learning Links." Becky explained that Collin's primary personality was outgoing, creative, highly social and energetic—very right brained. What he lacked was the ability to concentrate all that energy into a single focus. Through a three-month process of hand-eye coordination exercises, we saw an incredible change in our son.

His ability to understand math and spelling increased to the point of raising his grades within a few short weeks. Soon thereafter, Collin only needed reminding once or twice about his household chores—a far cry from his previous record.

Technically speaking, the exercises helped to integrate the left and right sides of the brain. No longer was Collin just a highly rambunctious little boy with a great personality; he could now intelligently connect with a problem and explore possible solutions.

Becky Kennard shares the following insight:

Statistics show that more than 50 percent of the population are visual learners rather than auditory learners.

Recent brain sequencing research proves the use of visual imagery, or right brain stimulation, enhances comprehension and storage recall effectively activating all modes of learning. Unfortunately in our churches we've bowed to worship at the altar of the spoken word but that's only half of God's plan for our lives.[10]

John Piper says, "God is most glorified in us when we are most satisfied with Him."

Once again this concept of different avenues of comprehension and learning reinforces Jesus' mode of parable teaching. Auditory learning is stored in our short-term memory whereas visual learning is stored in long-term memory. God desires to thrive in our long-term memory! That's where the Holy Spirit can produce the greatest results in transforming our souls.

To God Be the Glory

So how does God feel about all this hullabaloo surrounding worship expression? Listen to what John Piper says: "God is most glorified in us when we are most satisfied with Him."[11] God enjoys His people and loves to receive their worship in all forms. Don't let anyone tell you otherwise! Of all the vehicles of worship, what says it best? They all do. I'm forever searching for new ways and means to communicate the depths of my being to a God who experiences no boundaries and perceives no limits. I believe our deepest fulfillment in life is realized by searching and finding avenues to express our innermost longings to God.

Throughout history, there have been those who have pioneered and pointed the way to God by their lifestyles of passionate pursuit. We can read the accounts of those gone before and realize their contribution to the spiritual revelation we now enjoy. The path of holiness has been forged with great effort and pain and we are the blessed beneficiaries of this inheritance earned with the toil and tears of the saints. Lest we take for granted and treat lightly the rich heritage we now hold, let us take a walk down memory lane into the past of the patriarchs.

Notes

1. James Strong, *Strong's Exhaustive Concordance* (Nashville, Tenn.: Crusade Bible Publishers, Inc., 1983), #1984.
2. Robert E. Webber, *Worship Is a Verb* (Peabody, Mass.: Hendrickson Publishers, 1996), p. 45.
3. James Strong, #1804.
4. Ronald Gagne, *Introducing Dance in Christian Worship* (Washington, D.C.: The Pastoral Press, 1984), p. 59.
5. Bob Sorge, *Exploring Worship* (Canandaigua, N.Y.: Oasis House Publishers, 1987), p. 9.
6. Tim Keller, "What It Takes to Worship Well," *Leadership*, Spring 1994, pp. 17-23.
7. Robert E. Webber, *Worship Is a Verb*, p. 26.
8. Lora Allison, *Celebration: Banners, Dance and Holiness in Worship* (New Wilmington, Pa.: Sonrise Publications and Distribution, 1987), pp. 21-37.
9. Wade Harlan, "Capturing Hearts and Minds for Frontier Missions," *Mission Frontiers*, March-April 1997, pp. 8-9.
10. Becky Kennard, "Learning Links," Colorado Springs, Co.
11. John Piper, *Let the Nations Be Glad* (Grand Rapids, Mich.: Baker Books, 1996), p. 22.

WHERE HAVE WE BEEN?

*Faith of our fathers! Living still in spite of the
dungeon fire and sword:
Oh how our hearts beat high with joy when e'er we
hear that glorious word!
Faith of our fathers, holy faith! We will be true to
thee till death!*

"FAITH OF OUR FATHERS"
BY FREDERICK W. FABER, HENRI F. HEMY

(circa A.D. 33) Perhaps it was a day like so many other spring days in Jerusalem. The sky was partly cloudy with a hint of showers on the way. The townspeople, going about their daily chores, were buying food at the marketplace and drawing water from the local well for the day.

As instructed by Jesus upon His departure, the believers were gathered together to wait upon the Lord in a "house church" setting. All the disciples were there along with a host of others—about 120 altogether. For 10 days they stayed in the house ministering to the Lord in worship and prayer, actively "waiting" upon God.

Finally, when the day of Pentecost arrived, a strange and powerful phenomenon occurred. Suddenly a noise like heavy wind was heard from heaven and filled the whole house. As it passed by each person, little flames of fire undaunted by the wind were deposited upon the people's heads. At that moment, they were all filled with the Holy Spirit and began to speak in unknown languages as the Spirit flowed through them.

Being an appointed feast time, the city was heavily populated by many coming to celebrate. The sound of the holy wind was heard for blocks and people flocked from all around to see what in the world was going on as they heard the praise of God in their own language. What an awesome opportunity for Peter to preach this "good news" which added 3,000 to the newly birthed Church of Jesus Christ.

Flames of Faith Fanned in the Furnace of Affliction

This scene from Acts is a perfect picture of the divine destiny God has chosen for every tribe and nation through the New Covenant: to worship God in its own tongue, point unbelievers to Jesus and redeem the culture (see Acts 1:15 and 2:1-41).

Imagine this instantaneous "epiphany" experience. In that moment of spiritual enlightenment, all of life that holds enormous significance now pales in agonizing comparison to the glorious and supernatural awareness of God's visitation. To be found in that place of holy encounter, but for a moment, parallels the psalmist's confession, "A day in thy courts is better than a thousand outside" (Ps. 84:10).

It would be heaven on earth to live in that place of sacred awe forever. However, great heroes of the faith such as Oswald Chambers have inferred that God will see to it that we are not allowed to remain on the mountaintop. Those "rare" moments are reserved for God's discretion. We need the valleys to test those lessons of character learned on the mountaintop. In the furnace of affliction and persecution is where true faith is forged:

> Never live for the rare moments, they are surprises. God will give us touches of inspiration when He sees we are not in danger of being led away by them. We must never make our moments of inspiration our standard; our standard is our duty.[1]

The Persecuted Church

As the fledgling Church began to take its first yet strong steps, Satan opposed this new Christ religion, doing everything to dissuade it from reaching the known world with the gospel. Many did "not love their life even to death" (Rev. 12:11) as persecution reached unprecedented levels under the evil emperor Nero. His demonic and insane methods of torture and execution produced thousands of martyrs in the first-century Church. Still, the life of God could not be snuffed out.

Periodic severe persecution, including confiscation of property, imprisonment and violent death, over the following two centuries did little to kill the movement. The purpose of God was flourishing as the Church that was born in persecution now thrived in it. Then, at the beginning of the fourth century, Constantine became the new Roman emperor and officially embraced Christianity, bringing the age of the martyrs to an end.

Historians debate the extent to which Constantine's motives for converting were heartfelt or merely political. Nevertheless, Christianity then became the "compulsory" religion of a reforming empire. No longer persecuted by the government, the Church was now supported and patronized by it. The once "on guard," vigilant and prophetic Body of Jesus Christ was suddenly a mixed body of Christians and barely converted pagans— a huge challenge for the Church that had tremendously important ramifications. Western civilization was marked by many people who were "Christian" in name only.

For the next thousand years, there were always embers of holy fire stoked by men and women of God who knew a higher call to righteousness and holiness than what their current religious culture afforded. Men such as Athanasius (A.D. 295-373), who was instrumental in helping to maintain the orthodox teachings of Jesus Christ; Saint Augustine (A.D. 354-430), whose fundamental approach to God helped to shape modern-day theology; and later, Saint Francis of Assisi (A.D. 1181-1226), who renounced his wealth and took on a lifestyle intended to imitate that of the Lord Jesus.

Often rising from the grassroots of society, yet sometimes descending from the spire of status and wealth, these kinds of men and women were used of God to point back to the simplicity and purity of devotion to Christ (see 2 Cor. 11:3). Today we might blanch at some of their ascetic practices; however, the unique and fervent flavor of the approach to God represented in these precious few was a witness against the lukewarmness and spiritual complacency that often plagued the organized Church.

The Crusades

From the end of the eleventh to the middle of the fifteenth century, the Crusaders attempted to win the Holy Land from Islam, and to check the expanding Ottoman Empire. Part of the legacy of the Crusades is that Christians committed atrocities in the name of Christ against Jews, Muslims and even Eastern Orthodox Christians—atrocities that have never been forgotten. Because of the Crusaders' association with hatred and murder, the name of Christ and the sign of the cross became disdained in the very countries where Christianity had once flourished. The power and wealth of the Holy Roman Empire virtually replaced the need for power and revelation from God, reducing worship, once again, to a rigid set of dogma and cadaverous doctrine set in motion by ignorant, ambitious men. This abuse of power and authority is what fed the fire of the early reformers.

At least in part it seems that God did not allow the Holy Roman Empire to achieve a lasting victory in the Crusades. Rather He sought to teach the Church that military power and glory and wealth can never replace the Holy Spirit's power and revelation which comes out of right worship that is pleasing to God (see Zech. 4:6). Another factor in the Crusaders' demise is that despite exemplary individuals, terrible compromise and corruption infiltrated the Church. Ignorant, self-serving and greedy people eagerly abused their power and authority while Church practice tended to emphasize rituals, sacraments and unquestioning obedience. These factors in part set the stage for the Reformation of the sixteenth century.

The Reformation

One of the most important forerunners to the Reformation, the Englishman John Wycliffe, helped translate the Scriptures in a time of great turmoil in England's history. One historian writes:

> Irreversible seismic shifts were changing the patterns of life in fourteenth-century England. The Black Death, Hundred Years War, and the Peasants Revolt were dramatic symbols of a world in rapid transition.[2]

Wycliffe was considered a heretic by the religious leaders of the day. He maintained that the Bible should be the sole source of doctrine, and that no Church authorities could add to it. He challenged the Pope's claim as head of the Church, claiming that the Bible taught Christ had that office alone. He also attacked the doctrine of transubstantiation as superstitious.

Wycliffe translated the Bible from Latin into the language of the "common people." He was opposed by Church authorities during his lifetime, but it is amazing that 31 years after his death in 1415, the Council of Constance found him guilty on more than 200 counts of heresy and ordered his writings destroyed, his bones exhumed, burned and thrown into the river. Obviously,

Wycliffe's doctrines were very threatening to the existing Church authorities.

The sixteenth century brought the most famous protestant reformers to the spotlight. In Germany, Martin Luther heralded the message that faith alone justifies, apart from works. In Geneva, the Frenchman John Calvin was the primary catalyst for the revelation of God's sovereignty and irresistible grace. We can thank God for how the Reformation recovered essential biblical truths. However, the traditionalism of the Church became a big impediment to experiencing the power of the early New Testament Church they longed for.

The seventeenth century introduced new players on the world's stage of revival. The Puritan Movement tried to reform the Church of England, placing great emphasis on solid doctrines of the Scripture expanding the hearts of men to more truth, light and understanding. From this new intellectual and spiritual awareness of biblical teachings came the Congregational and the Baptist movements, each with their respective emphases on local church government and the importance of baptism by immersion.

At this strategic moment, with the *King James Version* of the Bible freshly completed, the Mayflower sailed to the New World laden with believers who envisioned the planting of a new colony based on worshiping God with heart and soul from the strength of the virtues they embraced.

The Great Awakening

The eighteenth century brought forth the first Great Awakening (1740-1742 at its peak). John and Charles Wesley, founders of the Methodists; George Whitefield, an evangelist who preached outdoors to thousands at a time; and Jonathan Edwards, one of the greatest thinkers and preachers this country has ever produced, made their debut as prominent spiritual leaders. Meanwhile, on the European continent, the Moravians began sending missionaries to the ends of the earth. George Frideric Handel composed

"Messiah," and Johann Sebastian Bach wrote his great music "to the glory of God." With the Great Awakening in full swing, the God-consciousness of Europe and America realized a dramatic increase as famous hymn writers of the century captured their faith in song. True and deeply spiritual conversions were expressed in the melodies of Isaac Watts and Charles Wesley that revolutionized the concept of hymn singing in church services.

In 1858 God visited the United States with a powerful outpouring of His Spirit. It is possible that the deposit of God's grace upon this nation at that time is what sustained it through the Civil War. The next year a similar move of God in Ulster in Wales spread swiftly to Scotland, then greatly affected England.

The progression of revelation from the eighteenth century increased through the nineteenth. The well-known ministries of George Mueller's orphanages and prayer, Charles Finney's evangelism, Dwight L. Moody's evangelism, Charles Spurgeon's preaching, and William and Catherine Booth's Salvation Army forged a path for the American Holiness Movement.

In addition, a surge of interest in divine healing was created by the ministries of Ethan Allen, Charles Cullis, the Keswick Movement, the Higher Life Movement, and other high-profile leaders. Marx's doctrines weren't really big until the twentieth century; most Christians didn't notice the naturalistic supposition of evolution and tried to reconcile biblical faith with evolution in the nineteenth century. If revival comes as a result of God's people asking for it, then we can see that God's commitment to answer prayers for revival in each subsequent generation becomes more apparent as the kingdom of God advances through numerous missions endeavors, contributing to the progress of spiritual recovery.

Holiness Churches

By the turn of the twentieth century, thousands of local Holiness congregations and dozens of Holiness sects and associations were formed in the South, Southwest and midwestern states. There was great hunger for something deeper and more tangible of the presence of God that would not only bring continuity to past revelation, but would also supersede previous moves of God. "Newness," "fresh fire" and "supernatural visitation" became the cry of those brave enough and humble enough to live on the edge of a new age beginning to dawn.

Seventy-five percent of those who came to Christ during the Welsh revival wandered into a meeting off the streets.

In 1901 some Bible School students in Topeka, Kansas, under the leadership of Charles Fox Parham, had a fresh visitation from the Lord. The Holy Spirit paid them a visit with a manifestation of speaking in tongues. This was the beginning of a new wave of experience that would soon sweep the world.

The Great Welsh Revival

The Great Welsh Revival, which began in 1903-4, was preceded by hungry hearts seeking the face of God for an outpouring of His Spirit. Evan Roberts, a prep school student and blacksmith apprentice, had a burning desire and a compulsion to see Wales won for Christ. Through his preaching and the demonstration of the Spirit, three things proved that God was with him: greatly increased church attendance, unity between different denominations and the "baptism of the Holy Spirit." According to the book of Acts, the purpose of Spirit baptism is power to be Christ's witnesses in all the earth (see 1:8). A powerful wave of conviction and repentance swept through the nation. Some reports say the crime rate dropped so dramatically that the local police had nothing to do—so they formed a gospel quartet.

Seventy-five percent of those who came to Christ during the Welsh revival wandered into a meeting off the streets. A report tells of a particular jail with only one prisoner who was ultimately led to the Lord. During his trial he gave his salvation testimony after which the jury sang the "Hallelujah Chorus."

The news of this revival traveled quickly to various parts of the hungry world. The momentum of the Spirit was increasing as He found willing participants to once again relinquish their hold on stale doctrine and receive a new spark of life.

The Azusa Street Revival

In April of 1905 a man in Los Angeles, California, by the name of Frank Bartleman was listening to a preacher describe the Great Revival in Wales. Mr. Bartleman was stirred to his core! He prayed that God would be pleased to use him to bring revival to Southern California. The Lord heard and answered those prayers. The ensuing months leading up to April 1906 were filled with travail and intercession for a revelation of God's presence. The glorious appearing took place gradually at the Azusa Street Mission. With initially only enough room for about 30 people to sit, people began to crowd into the small building and gather outside night after night to experience the phenomena of the Spirit's manifestations, including speaking and singing in unknown tongues.

April 18, 1906, the infamous San Francisco earthquake rumbled through Northern California, devastating the region and creating an awareness of spiritual need. People assumed God was judging the city. Mr. Bartleman writes:

> The San Francisco earthquake was surely the voice of God to the Pacific Coast. It was used mightily in conviction for the gracious after revival. In the early "Azusa" days both heaven and hell seemed to have come to town....A very

"dead-line" seemed to be drawn around the Azusa Mission by the Spirit. When men came within two blocks of the place they were seized with conviction.[3]

This move of revival swept the nation and the world from a little mission on Azusa Street in Los Angeles. The flame of holy passion lingered for the next decade and a half, producing an entire menagerie of new denominations, each with its individual grasp of a particular element of truth deposited through this revival. Many Pentecostal groups were formed which emphasized holiness as well as the gifts of the Holy Spirit with signs, wonders and miracles. The Azusa Street Revival and aftermath were a unique blend of previous moves of God combined with the fire of the "baptism in the Holy Spirit." Then, as with revival outbursts of the past, the need for men to institutionalize the movement caused the universal fire and passion for God to wane.

Latter Rain Movement

Nearly 50 years after Parham's Pentecostal experience in Topeka, Kansas, another cry for awakening reached the ears of God. Violet Kitely, a young widow and prophetic intercessor, was one who saw the serious need for fresh fire. In her words, "That which was born in the fire (of the turn of the century revival) was now just surviving in the smoke."[4] It was time for God to visit her generation.

In early February 1948, a group of 70 people, mostly students and farmers, assembled together at Sharon Bible School in North Battleford, Saskatchewan, Canada. The purpose of the gathering was to fast and pray alone with the Word of God for three days until the Lord spoke to them. After the third day, they reconvened to discuss what they heard from God. Two men in the meeting known as the Houghton brothers delivered a prophetic word that God was about to pour out a "Latter Rain" (which referred to the former rain outpouring of 1906) upon all flesh. Furthermore, God would restore the Tabernacle of David through worship and glorious praise (see Amos 9:11).

Following these initial meetings, the glory of God came down with an overwhelming release of signs, wonders, miracles and the gifts of the Spirit. Soon, people from around the world heard of this and came to North Battleford to see for themselves. The "Latter Rain" movement was actually named by the critics whereas those in the heart of the stream preferred to call it the "Restoration." Two marks of restoration in the movement were the reclamation of the gift of prophecy (see Eph. 4:11) and the laying on of hands by the prophetic presbytery (see 1 Tim. 4:14). Both were now utilized for releasing people into their call in the Body of Christ.

Proactive Praise

Existing below the radar of the mainstream and the evangelical press, these restoration churches enjoyed relative obscurity in their early years. During this time they began developing systematic teachings on biblical patterns for worship that produced a genuine grasp of the believer's priestly call to minister to the Lord. The meetings were characterized by *proactive* praise as contrasted by the previous revivals with *reactive* praise. The Azusa Street worship services relied completely on the Holy Spirit "moving" people to praise whereas the Latter Rain revelation challenged men to offer the "sacrifice" of praise. The decision and commitment to worship the Lord was met by unique manifestations of His presence. Spontaneous expressions of worship were common features in these meetings as songs would be sung in unknown tongues, followed by interpretation. Many songs came straight from the Scriptures, and people found the Psalms to be a powerful current hymnal.

While the restoration churches celebrated in intense worship gatherings, an offshoot of this stream of revival began functioning in an evangelistic mode that launched numerous itinerant ministries. Gordon Lindsay, William Brannam, T. L. Osborne, Tommy Hicks, David Nunn, William Freeman, David DuPlessis, A. A. Allen, Jack Coe, Oral Roberts, Kathryn Kuhlman and Kenneth Hagin began deliverance, healing and miracle rallies that touched countless thousands.

God Works Through Imperfect but Obedient Vessels

1948 was a benchmark year! The nation of Israel, the United Nations and the World Council of Churches were formed. Another parallel point of interest was the launching of Billy Graham's ministry. Gordon Lindsay established an organization called "The Voice of Healing." Its primary purpose was to report the miraculous events in these ministries. *The Voice of Healing* magazine and organization later became known as Christ for the Nations.

Freda Lindsay, the late Gordon Lindsay's widow, shares her personal insight:

Unfortunately toward the mid 1950's, popularity, power and prosperity took their toll on many ministries and some virtually "disappeared" from the public forefront.[5]

Though emotional extremes and excesses tended to occur at this time, almost 50 years later we are still seeing the positive benefits of how God used imperfect but obedient vessels to restore power and purity to His Church. Despite the problems, God was mostly getting a good name as people were being healed, delivered and set free by His awesome power. It was a witness to the truth that the gifts of the Spirit *are* for today!

This realization, this "anointing" of the Holy Spirit on His Church, has led to the formation of many groups, among whom I will name the Full Gospel Businessmen's Association (founded 1953) and the Charismatic Ecumenical Renewal (founded 1956) as significant.

In 1960, an Episcopal priest, Dennis Bennett, helped carry this anointing to the mainline denominations. Throughout the decade of the '60s, God did not forget the liturgical or "mainline" side of Christendom and opened His redemptive heart in a spiritual outpouring on Anglicans, Lutherans and Catholics. This historically unprecedented outpouring has dramatically affected mainline Christians worldwide.

We have learned over the past 30 years that no denomination is a wineskin that can contain the fullness of God. One way or another, He will prove Himself to be unconfined by the systems and philosophies of men that try to control Him. One way or the other, the Holy Spirit wants to bring His fullness to the whole Body of Christ.

The "Latter Rain Movement" has created a consistent flow of creativity in worship. What has transpired since that time has been a progressive awareness of God's priority for true worship to release His blessing of revelation. This has been especially true for various congregations "flowing" in that anointing since the late '50s.

Shiloh Christian Fellowship in Oakland, California, pastored by Violet Kitely until her recent retirement, is just one example of a pioneering "worship" church. She was present in North Battleford when the Spirit descended on the eve of the Latter Rain outpouring. Soon thereafter she began to teach the importance of "ministering to the Lord" (Acts 13:2).

Worship Symposiums

In April of 1976, Barry Griffing, worship leader at Shiloh, received a prophetic word about a "dual river" consisting of the Word and music that would flow and bless thousands in many churches. The following year, Barry attended a music conference at Bible Temple in Portland, Oregon, where the words of the prophet came back to him about this dual river. He then thought, *Why don't we have a worship conference for pastors, parishioners and appointed worshipers?*

The idea was approved by the Shiloh leaders and in August of 1978, the first "National Worship Conference" was held.

Although only 150 people registered, 40 out of 50 states were represented along with several international visitors. That year, Dave Moody's song "All Hail King Jesus" made its debut. People became so excited about the worship music, a sudden burst of new choruses started being written. Thus began the "Worship Symposium" concept that has continued through the '80s and into the '90s.

The International Worship Symposiums became a tool for worshiping churches (and those who wanted to be) to see and hear what the Spirit was saying to the churches in the area of creative art in worship. Not only were new worship songs discovered but qualified teachers were also available to instruct in the crafts of mime, dance and drama. Through the ensuing years, vision became realized as numerous ministries were launched upon the earth from the symposium platform that functioned as a clearinghouse for anointed creativity. Over a 20-year period, more than 30,000 people have attended one of these conferences, representing 10,000 churches!

Renewal

Exciting things were happening in other Christian music and worship circles as well around the same time. In the early '70s David and Dale Garret began publishing their music with Scripture in song while Bill and Gloria Gaither were piquing the Evangelical interest in worship with their heartfelt music. Maranatha! Music came into being, capturing the new youthful, vibrant sound of folk-rock-style worship. Maranatha! was one of the first recording companies to offer the Church contemporary worship music that was easily accessible for congregational use. From those studios came their "Praise" series which blessed the Church for 15 years.

Not long after Maranatha! Music became an entity, the sound of the Vineyard music was birthed through the musical gifts of the late John Wimber. Then in the early '80s, two men who had been associated with Bob Mumford and *New Wine* magazine had an experience with God in worship. They soon realized the need for live recorded worship services in the Christian market. So they answered a call from God to capture the element of live praise and worship on tape in 1985 by founding Integrity's Hosanna! Music.

It seemed the entire born-again world was experiencing a hunger for intimacy with God that could only be satisfied through the medium of worship. What better way to unite the Body of Christ than around the Cross and the throne! Through the efforts of several merging streams, the "Praise and Worship" renewal was born.

The '90s have brought new works of renewal. God is arranging things in His house and in the hearts of people that will accommodate another wave of His glory. The general consensus is that we are being primed for genuine revival in the land. As we anticipate another glorious appearing of our Lord Jesus Christ, our pursuit of Him through authentic worship expressions is strategic. We must see that we are "preparing the way of the Lord" as we worship Him.

With an understanding of history and what our forefathers did to prepare for the day of their visitation, our preparation through prophetic worship and intercession is casting up a highway and paving the road for Him to descend. So, clear the path, remove the stones! That is to say, "lay aside every encumbrance, and the sin which so easily entangles us, and let us run with endurance the race that is set before us" (Heb. 12:1).

Focusing on the Father's Goal

For those of you who enjoy jogging or marathon running, you realize the importance of setting a goal and pacing yourself to achieve it. Kingdom work is exactly the same. We must determine our goals and set a spiritual yet practical pace while we endeavor to pursue it.

If the goal is to receive the Father's love, then I must surround myself with things that contribute to that goal of intimacy.

If the goal is to be stronger in spirit to withstand the attacks of darkness, then I must ruthlessly wage war against those things while I lift the shield of faith. If the goal is to follow hard after Him, then I must set my heart to earnestly seek His face. In each of these areas and more, precedents are established by those who've achieved these goals; not taking advantage of their enlightenment would be a waste of their experience.

The same holds true in the arena of worship. What God is doing around the globe in worship is truly remarkable. As technology increases we are able to access virtually every kind of worship music style and expression available. To understand the full counsel of God, we need to hear what He's saying to others with similar callings and heart motivations. The goal is to know Him and make Him known, so let's do our homework to find out how others have achieved this goal.

Notes

1. Oswald Chambers, *My Utmost For His Highest* (Uhrichsville, Ohio: Barbour and Company, Inc., 1935), p. 88.
2. "Wycliffe's England: A Time of Turmoil," *Christian History*, Vol. II, No. 2, Issue 3, (Carol Stream, Ill.: *Christianity Today*, 1998), pp. 6-9.
3. Frank Bartleman, *Another Wave Rolls In* (Northridge, Calif.: Voice Christian Publications, Inc., 1962), p. 54.
4. Violet Kitely, Shiloh Christian Fellowship, Oakland, Calif. (telephone interview, December 2, 1997).
5. Freda Lindsay, Christ for the Nations Institute, Dallas, Tex. (telephone interview, December 11, 1997).

START WHERE YOU ARE

Just as I am,
Without one plea but that Thy blood was shed for me,
And that Thou biddst me come to Thee,
Oh Lamb of God, I come! I come!

"JUST AS I AM"
BY CHARLOTTE ELLIOTT AND WILLIAM B. BRADBURY

"Frasier of Lisuland in Northern Burma translated the Scriptures into the Lisu language and then left a young fellow with the task of teaching the people to read.

When he returned six months later, he found three students and the teacher seated around a table, with the Scriptures opened in front of the teacher. When the students each read, they left the Bible where it was. The man on the left read it sideways, the man on the right read it sideways but from the other side, and the man across from the teacher read it upside down. Since they always occupied the same chairs, that's how each had learned to read, and that's how each thought the language was written.

We, too, can be like that. When we learn something from only one perspective, we may think it's the only perspective.

Sometimes it's good to change seats to assume a different perspective on the same truth."[1]

Worship is not a divine duty; it is a divine devotion birthed out of sacrificial love.

A Heavenly Perspective

When Jesus came to earth, He changed seats with us and took on all our sin, rejection and shame so we could see ourselves from His perspective. The Bible says, "But God, being rich in mercy, because of His great love with which He loved us, even when we were dead in our transgressions, made us alive together with Christ (by grace you have been saved), and raised us up with Him, and *seated us with Him in the heavenly places,* in Christ Jesus" (Eph. 2:4-6, italics added).

Why did He seat us in heavenly places? So we could see worship from His perspective. Worship is not a divine duty; it is a divine devotion birthed out of sacrificial love.

When Jesus went to the cross, the Scriptures tell us that "one of the soldiers pierced His side with a spear, and immediately there came out blood and water" (John 19:34). Not only had the veil been torn in the Temple, allowing us to enter the holy of holies, but the sack around the Father's heart was also torn so we might see His love for us and drink from the living water that surrounds His heart.

Oh to be a true worshiper! Philippians 3 has much to say about true worship. It begins with a warning to beware of the "false circumcision" (v. 2) and reminds us that we are the "true circumcision" who worship in the "Spirit of God" and "put no confidence in the flesh" (v. 3). In other words, we don't worship any longer based on outward appearances; we worship in the Spirit of God. It doesn't matter what outer clothing we adorn ourselves with or how spiritual we may look by our physical stance (i.e., lifting our hands or closing our eyes); what matters is that our hearts have been circumcised.

It is completely possible to wear a $500 suit or a $300 dress and have a heart that is dressed in the soiled rags of unforgiveness, jealousy and judgment. Our goal in worship is not to impress others; it is to experience the presence of the Father.

The Redeeming Presence of God

First Chronicles 13 tells the story of David bringing the Ark of the Covenant back to Jerusalem on an ox-drawn cart. Through ignorance and disobedience, one of David's servants, Uzza, died while trying to steady the Ark. In disgrace and disillusionment, David then placed the Ark in the home of Obed-edom for three months so he could research the prescribed method for escorting the Lord's presence, which turned out to be the shoulders of the priests rather than the back of an ox. For the ox represents "works."

I find it phenomenal that the Lord God would allow His temporary dwelling place (the Ark) to rest in the home of Obed-edom. One might think it was just a fluke of chance that this man's house was chosen for the presence of God. But I believe the Lord desired to make a point in history about His desire toward humanity by placing it there. You see, Obed-edom's name is derived from two words: "Obed," meaning "to serve" and "Edom," a descendant of Esau, related to Adam who was earth, earthly and the epitome of the flesh.

By dwelling in the home of this "servant of the flesh," God chose to prove His heart of redemption for all those who have failed in their attempts to find God through fleshly efforts. Though we may have responded to God in a fleshly way, He shows us that there is hope for righting the wrong by abiding with us. If we can receive the embrace of God in the midst of trauma, we can be assured that devastating situations in life do not have to mar us forever.

What About You?

Are you feeling as though you have failed the Lord in your personal or corporate worship? Take comfort from the words of the apostle Paul who said, "I do not regard myself as having laid hold of it yet; but one thing I do: forgetting what lies behind and reaching forward to what lies ahead, I press on toward the goal for the prize of the upward call of God in Christ Jesus" (Phil. 3:13,14).

I recently received the following poem which speaks to all who have endured the shame of falling, stumbling and wanting to quit. I share it with you as a reminder that we do not run this race for others but for the Father who sees our failures and loves us in spite of them.

The Race

"Quit!" "Give up, you're beaten,"
They shout and plead;
"There's just too much against you now,
This time you can't succeed."

And as I start to hang my head
In front of failure's face,
My downward fall is broken
By the memory of a race.

And hope refills my weakened will
As I recall that scene.
For just the thought of that short race
Rejuvenates my being.

A children's race, young boys, young men;
Now I remember well...
Excitement, sure, but also fear;
It wasn't hard to tell.

They all lined up so full of hope,
Each thought to win that race;
Or tie for first, or if not that,
At least take second place.

And fathers watched from off the side,
Each cheering for his son.
And each boy hoped to show his dad
That he would be number one.

The whistle blew and off they went,
Young hearts and hopes on fire.
To win, to be the hero there,
Was each young boy's desire.

And one boy in particular,
His dad was in the crowd,
Was running near the lead and thought,
"My dad will be so proud."

But as he speeded down the field,
Across a shallow dip,
The little boy who thought to win,
Lost his step and slipped.

Trying hard to catch himself,
His hands flew out to brace,
And mid the laughter of the crowd,
He fell flat on his face.

So down he fell and with him hope,

He couldn't win it now.
Embarrassed, sad, he only wished
To disappear somehow.

But as he fell, his dad stood up
And showed his anxious face,
Which to the boy so clearly said,
"Get up and win that race!"

He quickly rose, no damage done,
Behind a bit, that's all,
And ran with all his mind and might
To make up for his fall.

So anxious to restore himself,
To catch up and to win,
His mind went faster than his legs.
He slipped and fell again.

He wished that he had quit before
With only one disgrace.
"I'm hopeless as a runner now,
I shouldn't try to race."

But in the laughing crowd he searched
And found his father's face...
That steady look that said again,
"Get up and win that race."

So he jumped up to try again,
Ten yards behind the last,
"To gain those yards," he thought,
"I've got to run real fast."

Exceeding everything he had,
He regained eight or ten,

But trying hard to catch the lead,
He slipped and fell again.

Defeat! He lay there silently,
A tear dropped from his eye.
"There's no sense running anymore.
Three strikes, I'm out—why try!"

The will to rise had disappeared,
All hope had fled away.
So far behind, so error prone,
Closer all the way.

"I've lost, so what's the use," he thought,
"I'll live with my disgrace."
But then he thought about his dad;
Who soon he'd have to face.

"Get up," an echo sounded low.
"Get up and take your place.
You're not meant for failure here,
Get up and win that race."

With borrowed will, "Get up," it said,
"You haven't lost at all...
For winning's nothing more than this:
To rise each time you fall."

So up he rose to win once more.
And with a new commit,
He resolved that win or lose,
At least he wouldn't quit.

So far behind the others now,
the most he'd ever been.

Still he gave all he had to give
And ran as though to win.

Three times he'd fallen, stumbling,
Three times he rose again.
Too far behind to hope to win,
He still ran to the end.

They cheered the winning runner
As he crossed, first place,
Head high and proud and happy;
No falling, no disgrace.

But when the fallen youngster
Crossed the line, last place,
The crowd gave him the greater cheer
For finishing the race.

And even though he came in last,
With head bowed low, unproud,
You would have though he won the race,
To listen to the crowd.

And to his dad he sadly said,
"I didn't do so well."
"To me you won," his father said,
"You rose each time you fell."

And now when things seem dark and hard
And difficult to face,
The memory of that little boy
Helps me in my race.

For all of life is like that race,
With ups and downs and all,

And all you have to do to win
Is rise each time you fall.

"Quit! Give up; you're beaten,"
They still shout in my face.
But another voice within me says,
"Get up and finish the race."
—Author Unknown

What about your race? Let's get up, let's start over together...

Lord, please come and bring renewed vision for a healthy relationship with You. I confess all my past failures in private worship and my lack of desire to follow hard after You. I also confess my present fears of slipping again when I lose focus of you. I now choose to believe that You are interested in my life as an offering of worship. So I invite you to change those things in my heart that always search for the easiest way to gain the most out of my life. Lord, help me see through eyes of faith that the reward for those who earnestly seek You is nothing less than Your presence. There really is nothing greater than that. As inexperienced as I may be, I need You to coach me through this "lifestyle of worship" idea. Today, I present myself to You as willing to be changed. In Jesus' name. Amen.

Note
1. Craig Brian Larson, *Illustrations for Preaching and Teaching* (Grand Rapids, Mich.: Baker Books, 1993), p. 179.

BIBLIOGRAPHY

Allison, Lora. *Celebration: Banners, Dance and Holiness in Worship*. New Wilmington, Pa.: Sonrise Publishing and Distribution, 1987.

Bartleman, Frank. *Another Wave Rolls In*. Northridge, Calif.: Voice Christian Publications, Inc., 1962.

Bennet, Peter and Dorothy. *Just Water Under the Bridge?*. Llanfairfechan, Gwynedd, Wales: Chattham House, 1995.

Blomgren, David K., Dean Smith, Douglas Christoffel. *Restoring Praise and Worship to the Church*. Shippensburg, Pa.: Revival Press, 1989.

——. *Song of the Lord*. Portland, Oreg.: Bible Press, 1978.

Brant, Roxanne. *Ministering to the Lord*. Springdale, Pa.: Whitaker House, 1993.

Bridges, Jerry. *The Pursuit of Holiness*. Colorado Springs, Colo.: Navpress, 1978.

Book of Common Prayer, Episcopal. Kingsport, Tenn.: Kingsport Press, for Church Hymnal Corp., 1977.

Book of Common Worship/Daily Prayer. Louisville. Ky.: Westminster/John Knox Press, 1993.

Boschman, LaMar. *The Prophetic Song*. Bedford, Tex.: Revival Press, 1986.

——. *A Passion for His Presence*. Shippensburg, Pa.: Destiny Image Publishing, Inc., 1992.

——. *The Rebirth of Music*. Little Rock, Ark.: Manasseh Books, 1980.

Carter, T. P. *Jokes, Notes and Quotes*. Columbus, Ga.: Quill Publications, 1991.

Chambers, Oswald. *My Utmost for His Highest*. Uhrichsville, Ohio: Barbour and Company Inc., 1935.

Christian History.

    Vol. II, No. 2, Issue 3

    Vol. IX, No. 1, Issue 25; No.4, Issue 28

    Vol. X, No. 3, Issue 31

    Vol. XII, No. 2, Issue 38

    Vol. XIII, No. 2, Issue 42; No. 3, Issue 43

    Vol. XIV, No. 1, Issue 45; No. 3, Issue 47; No. 4, Issue 4

    Vol. XVI, No. 1, Issue 53; No. 2, Issue 54

The Complete Library of Christian Worship. Nashville, Tenn.: Starsong Publishing Group, 1993.

Cornwall, Judson. *Let Us Diet.* England: Sharon Publications, Ltd., 1990.

——. *Let Us Praise.* Logos International, 1973.

Cruden, Alexander. *Cruden's Complete Concordance.* Philadelphia, Pa.: The John C. Winston Company, 1949.

Davis, Marietta. *Scenes Beyond the Grave.* Dallas, Tex.: Christ for the Nations, Inc., 1980 reprint.

Dawson, John. *Taking Our Cities for God.* Lake Mary, Fla.: Creation House, 1989.

Dawson, Joy. *Intimate Friendship with God Through Understanding the Fear of the Lord.* Grand Rapids, Mich.: Chosen Books, 1986.

Edwards, Gene. *The Divine Romance.* Auburn, Maine: Christian Books Publishing House, 1984.

Fry, Steve. *A God Who Heals the Heart.* Brentwood, Tenn.: Deep Fryed Books, 1997.

Gagne, Ronald, Thomas Kane, Robert VerEecke. *Introducing Dance in Christian Worship.* Washington, D.C.: The Pastoral Press, 1984.

Goss, Ethel. *The Winds of God.* Hazelwood, Mo.: Word Aflame Press, 1958.

Gruen, Earnest J. *Touching the Heart of God.* Springdale, Pa.: Whitaker House, 1986.

Hayford, Jack, John Killinger, Howard Stevenson. *Mastering Worship.* Portland, Oreg.: Multnomah Press, 1990.

Heflin, Ruth. *Glory—A Jerusalem Experience.* Hagerstown,

Md.: McDougal Publishing Company, 1990.

Jacobs, Cindy. *The Voice of God.* Ventura, Calif.: Regal Books, 1995.

———. *Possessing the Gates of the Enemy.* Grand Rapids, Mich.: Chosen Books, 1991.

Keller, Tim. "*What It Takes to Worship Well,*" *Leadership,* Spring 1994.

Kendrick, Graham. *Learning to Worship As a Way of Life.* Minneapolis, Minn.: Bethany House Publishers, 1984.

———. *Public Praise.* Altamonte Springs, Fla.: Creation House, 1992.

Kraeuter, Tom. *Worship Is...What?!* Lynnwood, Wash.: Emerald Books, 1996.

Larson, Craig Brian. *Illustrations for Preaching and Teaching.* Grand Rapids, Mich.: Baker Books, 1993.

———. *Contemporary Illustrations for Preachers, Teachers and Writers.* Grand Rapids, Mich.: Baker Books, 1996.

Law, Terry. *The Power of Praise and Worship.* Tulsa, Okla.: Victory House Publishers, 1985.

London, H. B. Jr. *Refresh, Renew, Revive.* Colorado Springs, Colo.: Focus on the Family Publishing, 1996.

Miller, L. David. *Hymns: The Story of Christian Song.* Philadelphia, Pa.: Lutheran Church Press, 1969.

McMinn, Don. *The Practice of Praise.* Word Music, 1992.

Murchison, Anne. *Praise and Worship in Earth As It Is in Heaven.* Dallas, Tex.: Word Books, 1981.

Murray, Andrew. *Abide in Christ.* Springdale, Pa.: Whitaker House, 1979.

———. *Loving God with All Your Heart.* Ann Arbor, Mich.: Vine Books, 1996.

New American Standard Bible. La Habra, Calif.: The Lockman Foundation, 1960, 1962, 1963, 1968, 1971, 1972, 1973, 1975, 1977.

Nouwen, Henri. *The Way of the Heart.* New York: Ballantine Books, 1981.

Piper, John. *Let the Nations Be Glad.* Grand Rapids, Mich.: Baker Books, 1996.

Riss, Richard. *Latter Rain*. Mississuaga, Ontario, Canada: Honeycomb Visual Productions, LTD., 1987.

Roget's International Thesaurus. New York: Thomas Y. Crowell Company, 1962.

Shaw, Gwen R. *Day by Day*. Jasper, Ark.: Engeltal Press, 1987.

Sheets, Dutch. *Intercessory Prayer*. Ventura, Calif.: Regal Books, 1996.

Sheets, Tim. *Heaven Made Real*. Shippensburg, Pa.: Destiny Image Publishers, Inc., 1996.

Sonmore, Clayt. *Beyond Pentecost*. Minnetonka, Minn.: Thy Kingdom Come Ministries, 1964.

Sorge, Bob. *Exploring Worship*. Canandaigua, N.Y.: Oasis House Publishers, 1987.

———. *In His Face*. Canandaigua, N.Y.: Oasis House Publishers, 1994.

Strong, James. *Strong's Exhaustive Concordance*. Nashville, Tenn.: Crusade Bible Publishers, Inc., 1983.

Truscott, Graham. *The Power of His Presence*. Burbank, Calif.: World Map Press, 1969.

Urang, Gunnar. *Church Music...For the Glory of God*. Moline, Ill.: Christian Service Foundation, 1956.

Voice of the Vineyard magazine. Anaheim, Calif.: Association of Vineyard Churches; Fall, 1997.

Webber, Robert E. *Worship Is a Verb*. Peabody, Mass.: Hendrickson Publishers, 1996.

Wilbur, Paul. *Make His Praise Glorious*. Colorado Springs, Colo.: Paul Wilbur Ministries, 1992.

Winslow, Tamara. *Praise and Worship*. Tamara Winslow Publishers, 1992.

———. *Song of the Lord*. Eastbourne, E. Sussex: Kingsway Publishers, 1996.

Use These Books to Encourage Yourself and Others

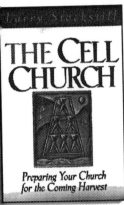
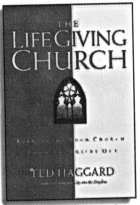
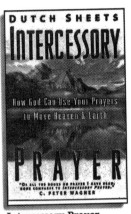
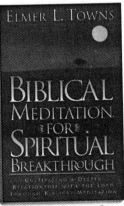
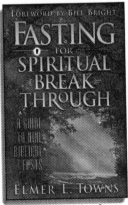
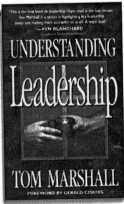